D1273292

1

This book is   dedicated

to my wife and children, they are my motivation in

everything that I do. I would gladly lay my life down on the

line for any one of them at any given time without a

second thought. Through their love and support

I have the privilege of experiencing

"Heaven on Earth"

on a daily

basis.

About the author

Brandon Thomas Crawford is an extremely accomplished man. At the age of 42, alongside his loving wife, Tonica Crawford, he has accumulated an admirable portfolio of investment properties. He founded Kingz LLC, Crawford Properties LLC and Crawford Construction & Contracting Corp. His welcoming demeanor and free spirit may suggest that he comes from a life of privilege but that couldn't be further from the truth.

Even as an infant the cards seemed to be stacked against Brandon. His mother died shortly after his birth from delivery complications. His father, defeated from the loss of the woman he loved, vowed to raise Brandon with little to no help. Brandon's father, Thomas Crawford, was in his 50's when his youngest son, Brandon was born. Amid all these broken hearts there lay a baby in desperate need of love, surrounded by damaged individuals who were mourning the loss of the beautiful, charismatic, unforgettable Pamela Dudley.

During Brandon's childhood and into adulthood, he proved to be an overachiever. This sort of extreme attention to detail and profound ability to anticipate the needs of others won him favor with almost everyone he encountered. This tactic served a dual purpose, Brandon was also able to conceal the fact that he yearned for unconditional love.

These psychological voids exist in many black men today and usually go undetected. As adults with unresolved feelings of abandonment and disregard its common to see men with uncontrollable anger or abusive, destructive behaviors. Our young men are told to "man up" amid pivotal moments of their lives. These are "hard times" in which they need the guidance of an attentive mother or father or both to have a chance at surviving the statistical outcome so many young men fall victim to.

Unable to recognize his true gift of teaching and innate ability to love without limits he eventually found comfort in the "street life". Brandon has spent almost twenty years behind bars. He has had to sit back and watch as close friends and family members have faded to black, with little to no contact.

This is a reality for over 2.2 Million Black men in America today.

Brandon received 4 nearly consecutive prison sentences all for Non-violent Drug Offenses. The end of each prison term marked the birth of a new man. Sitting at the tables studying Real Estate, Construction Management, Accounting and the history of Money in grave detail is where he could be found during this most recent incarceration. His study habits were so intense that he began to draw crowds and even teach unwittingly. With his magnetic personality and willingness to help anyone he created meaningful connections at every facility he was assigned to.

Brandon is the proud father of 9 children, Shilyn Crawford, the oldest, whom he adores and still as an adult and mother herself refers to as his "Princess Shi-baby". Brandon and Braijon Crawford, the only boys, who are both true reflections of their father's leadership and creative abilities. Honesty Crawford, the sweetest, she is a spitting image of her father and a sweet reminder of all that is good in the world. Kashauna Crawford, "The General" has a special place in her father's heart because he can relate to her the most. Avaya "Aviator" Mitchell, the brain, she is going to take our family name and business to uncharted heights, Aylah "The Bee" Mitchell, the intellectual, she melts her father's heart with just a smile, and lastly, Andrea and

Dominance Crawford, the babies of the crew, they are equally a sum total of the best parts of all of us combined!

Our beautiful "Love Story" that inspired all the greatness that has occurred over the past five years, was born just 6 months prior to Brandon's release from his 10-year mandatory sentence. Like a thief in the night, I stole his heart and willingly gave him mine. We fell in love immediately. I'm convinced that our love is the kind of love that the great poets wrote about. The love that we found in one another we would deny its very existence if we had not experienced it for ourselves. Our lives' missions have become unified. Through our union we mastered the ability of being two places at once. We got married the day he came home from prison within hours of his release. Our marriage was consummated that evening and our "love child" was conceived. Brandon, during his 10-year sentence earned his license in Barbering and became the staff barber at Belmont Correctional Institution in Belmont, Ohio.

Once released, he cut hair out of his bookbag in the projects, on porches or wherever he could access power outlets. He hustled his way to the top. I remember driving 30 miles to bring him dinner because he was in the kitchen of someone's house cutting head after head, grinding until his feet and hands gave out. Although his efforts were admirable eventually the cold reality of what it took to raise a family in this society with the stigma of a "felon" took hold and limited our opportunities. Criminal thinking and associations were not far off. After 18 months of freedom with his loving wife and newfound legit success his parole was violated and revoked for having a firearm in our home. Brandon was sentenced to 4 years in prison.

This time would soon become the "turning point in his life" the time when he realized his purpose and true mission in life which you will read about shortly. Not only did this time change Brandon but it defined the love and life we had built. Now, without the physical presence of my "Hero", my "Provider", my "Knight in Shining Armor" I encountered the harsh reality that I must face and conquer the world alone.

To my surprise, from inside the "belly of the beast" my husband has held my hand and taught me to manage and scale our businesses to heights I couldn't have imagined. Today we are equally yoked and that is something that will change the course of our lives.

For the first time in his life, Brandon is not returning home to a family that he must take care of, instead we are a family that is eagerly awaiting his brilliant contributions to the empire that we have already built TOGETHER.

Mission Statement

I will seek to balance business and family as best as I can since they are both important to me.

My home will be a place where not only I, but my family, friends and guest find joy, comfort, peace and happiness. I will exercise wisdom in what I choose to eat, read, see and do at home. I especially want to teach my children through my actions to love, learn and laugh and to be the best of themselves with each step that they take in life. I will do whatever that is in my scope of influence to help guide them to the God within their being.

I will value my wife with my life! I am the King of my world which makes her the Queen. Together we make up the body of god in the flesh, within our love lies the building blocks of all creation. I will honor my wife and our marriage as priority number one in my life because we are one.

I will value the rights, freedoms, beliefs and responsibilities of our communities. I will be a leader who walks the walk of his morals, values and beliefs that are in alignment with the universal law of God. I will be a concerned and informed community leader. I will become involved with the political process to ensure my voice is heard and my vote is counted.

I will be a self-made individual that will attack my life's goals with passion, vigor and love. I will act on situations and opportunities, rather than be acted upon.

I will always try to keep myself free from addictive and destructive habits. I will develop habits that free me from old labels. Labels that may cause me to form alter-ego's that control my decision making based off the acceptance of others.

My money will be my servant, not my master! My money will be assigned the task of making itself grow through my financial intelligence based off educating and serving others. My morals, values, beliefs, and universal principles will be the driving force behind every dollar that I make as well as every step that I take.

True greatness will be achieved through the abundant mind that works unselfishly with mutual respect for mutual benefit.

~Brandon T. Crawford

Table of Contents

Foreword

My husband is truly a gift to this world. Brandon T. Crawford has found his purpose in life as a "bridge to the youth". By using the term "bridge" as a description, we want to encompass Brandon's unique ability to reach communities of people who would otherwise be thrown to the wolves and disregarded as incorrigible. The previous statement covers one side of the" bridge" and at the other side of this hypothetical "bridge" lies an entry way to the world of privilege and unfair advantage.

By tirelessly studying Barron's Dictionaries of Real Estate Terms; Accounting; Finance and Investment Terms; along with hundreds of other books he now fluently speaks the language of money, although hood and street talk is his native tongue. Through his experience and teaching he has dedicated his life to reaching back to his community and those revered as "undesirables" to share this secret education. Brandon's mentor, Robert Kiyosaki, whose teachings you will see referenced throughout this book is an extremely successful businessman and author. Through Robert's books he provides financial and business education. This is the influence we wish to have on you through our first book, "The Secret Education of the Rich"

Although we have made the decision to release this valuable informative book of secrets to the public, originally my husband wrote this book as an instructional guide for our nine children, Shilyn, Brandon, Braijon, Honesty, Kashauna, Avaya, Aylah, Andrea, Dominance, and our granddaughter, Legaci. This alone should give you an idea of the love and passion that went into writing this. The decision to publish this book and make it available to the world was an easy one to make. Upon rereading the finished product, we were able to grasp the enormous opportunity we have, to not only influence, but contribute to generations to come through the fruits of my husband's twenty plus years of studying wealth acquisition.

The impact statements and book reviews displayed on the back cover are written by just a few of the many people whose lives Brandon has not only touched but transformed through his teachings and rare confidence in the potential of anyone he encounters. I am not surprised when my husband is addressed as a mentor, a teacher, or an inspiration just to name a few. Despite the consecutive trials he has experienced throughout his life on any given day he still defines his life as "heaven on earth!"

Brandon was born a motherless child. Brandon's beautiful mother Pamela Marie Combs died shortly after Brandon's birth as a result of complications due to delivery. Brandon's father Thomas "Ben Heinz" Crawford was in his 50's when Brandon was born. From the beginning of his life Brandon was set to walk a different path than most. Through his upbringing he was constantly driven by his father to "be a man," Brandon often refers to himself as a "man's man" which is truly who he is. I've witnessed him reinvent himself repeatedly during the course of our marriage and through reflection I see that he has also done this many other times throughout his life.

To talk about Brandon without mentioning the importance of the two concepts "assets" and "liabilities" is impossible. In the Crawford household we have made these two concepts the lens' through which we assess material items, people and situations. I know that our children will have the "unfair advantage" we now offer to you and your children, through this method of self and life evaluation.

His contributions to this world have been countless already. However, as my husband, my muse and my greatest supporter he has encouraged me in everything that I have done. Together we have built a Real Estate Empire that provides for our family. My husband and I founded Crawford Construction and Contracting Corp. in 2018 and in our first year transitioned to an S-Corporation due to our rapid growth. My husband is a Barber, by trade, together we founded Kingz LLC, a barbershop which we still own and operate in our hometown of Steubenville, Ohio. Although my husband has no intention of utilizing his extraordinary barbering skills, we currently use our barbershop as a place where rehabilitated felons or anyone with license can build a lucrative business for themselves through our weekly chair rental offer. With just a few words from a communication between my husband and I, I invite you inside the connection we share that allows us to give freely of ourselves to you and to the world...

"My love, you are Victorious! The battles that lay ahead of you are already won, my love. So, take every step fearlessly, because nothing that comes in your path shall prosper!! You will defeat and overcome any obstacle with just a blink of your eye!!! The only thing that you need to do is believe in yourself and know that the power that you hold right in the palm of your being is enough. You are the builder and destroyer of all things. Your word shall be done, and it will be written in stone for you are the goddess of all worlds and all things will bow at your feet when you speak. You must know this for the world to work the way that it was intended to work, everyone must play their position for this engine to run in harmony with itself. You are the key to life and its time that you play your position in every step that you take, you are Victorious!!!!!!!!!!!!!!"

This is the sort of unwavering belief that Brandon has not only in me, but in humanity. Allow this priceless information within these pages to stick with you and guide your steps as you embark on a journey of self-discovery and self-love through the eyes of the man I love most, Brandon Thomas Crawford.

Tonica Crawford

CEO of Crawford Construction & Contracting Corp.
Co-Founder and Owner of Crawford Properties & Kingz, LLC

Introduction

Money Master

This book that you have picked up has the potential to challenge everything you have ever been taught about money. I do not claim to be an expert. Although, I have put in over 10,000 hours of studying. Without blinking an eye, I can confidently tell you I am a Master regarding money. I speak and understand it fluently. I have worked tirelessly for over twenty years to acquire the knowledge you will find within these pages.

Originally this manuscript was written to be passed down to my children as *"The Marathon Continues"*, as the late Nipsy Hussle would say. Once I have fulfilled my purpose in this life and served as a bridge to the youth, my children will be left to carry the torch. I wrote this book with an open heart and a free mindset.

I packed a lot of information into the beginning of this book and more of the procedural information and reflections toward the end. My goal is to familiarize you with this transition into a wealthy mindset, then help you with a game plan on how to execute! I will introduce you to things like:

- The Origin of Money
- The Crawford Method
- WAHM

If there is anything that you struggle to comprehend, trust me, continue to read through it will all make sense as you begin to put the pieces together for yourself. I will give you the game, but I can't play it for you. First, let me start with the two most vital concepts of financial education: Assets and Liabilities.

Assets and Liabilities

Assets are the things that you purchase, acquire, encounter or create that put money into your pocket. (Investment properties, businesses, cash on hand, land, a trained and assembled workforce, a great smile, etc.)

Liabilities can also be things that you purchase, acquire, encounter or create that take money out of your pocket (Bills, Car payments, family members who borrow money from you and never repay you, car rims, clothes, a bad attitude, etc.)

Assets and liabilities do not just apply to finances. Many of us have children who are liabilities, specifically because they take money out of our pockets. It's our job to make them understand the need for financial education so that they can grow to become assets.

How to Use Assets and Liabilities

I know the first question is:

How can you productively use liabilities if they take money out of your pocket?

Well I never said that you could not enjoy liabilities. You just need more assets than liabilities so that you don't have more money coming out of your pocket than what is coming into it. Don't ever forget when you become wealthy you can live your life to the fullest. Then, money problems will be the least of your worries. Just so you know, I'm not preaching save money, my sermon is to acquire assets that so that you can enjoy your liabilities without the worries of going broke.

How to Use Assets

Assets can come in many forms. You can create an asset like Bill Gates, when he invented Microsoft. He took an idea and turned it into an asset. This idea turned asset made him a billionaire. Many people have billion-dollar ideas that can become assets if they are applied. Bill Gates didn't just have this idea pop in his head and then went on about his day like everyone else, he transformed that idea into an asset by taking his idea to the tech giant of his time IBM and structuring a deal to make him the richest man on the planet for nearly 2 decades. He utilized his asset to create wealth.

G.E.B. Board

Our current school system doesn't teach financial education. This is not by circumstance either; our education system was designed this way by the Elite (the rich). It was designed to build an army of worker bees. This army of worker bees are what's known as the middle class. In 1903, John D Rockefeller started what is called the G.E.B (General Education Board). He established the G.E.B board with only one purpose in mind: to build an army of worker bees. This was to produce an engine that would fund both, his and other elite players' goals, such as Andrew Carnegie, Paul Wahlberg, the Rothschilds, and the list goes on and on. This plot even formed the Federal Reserve, which is a complete book I could write, in and of itself.

{Ref: *The Creature from Jekyll Island by Edward G Griffin*}

Let's bring things back to this deceitful education system. You, me and our beautiful children have been targeted to be slaves in the system for the rest of our lives as well as generations and generations after us. While President Trump's son, Barron, is taught by billionaires and multimillionaires who don't care about being paid teacher wages, he is being taught financial education at its highest level. He's being groomed from birth to be the leader of the New World. Meanwhile, our children will be taught a Prussian education by teachers who live just above the poverty line. Think about this for a moment: It's almost impossible for a teacher who is a paycheck away from being in poverty to teach our children to become millionaires, let alone billionaires. Financial Literacy is basically nonexistent in our school's curriculums.

A Molded Mind

Let's quickly take a tour of this Prussian school system. From ages 3 to 5 years old, we are taught the basics, which I agree, are essential for our growth and development in early years from birth, for example: colors, alphabet, numbers and language. What most average people, the worker bees, don't know is that these are vital years for our children. Their brains are like sponges until their teenage years. They are capable of retaining the most complex formulas and teachings. When we make the decision to accept only the basic teachings for children from the ancient school system, we are intentionally limiting our children's growth potential. In the meantime, at the White House, young Barron is not only learning more than the basics at school, but at home he is hearing, watching and seeing his father and mother as well as his siblings making power move after power move. His family runs a billion-dollar enterprise in many factions of real estate and business. He has also seen his father position himself to be the President of the United States, where he now runs the world economy of finance. President Trump is not the president by accident. Personally, people may hate our President but financially he is a genius; and this is exactly why he is the president. We have yet to see what the future holds for Barron, although we know that the odds are in his favor. Now let's look in our own homes and reflect on what our children are hearing, watching and seeing.

Humble Beginnings

I came from a single-parent home. My mother died from delivery complications in the hospital shortly after giving birth to me, she was only 23 years old. My father was a 50-year-old who could barely read and write. The things that I heard, watched and saw were completely different from what young Barron was exposed to. I grew up and what was commonly known as a crack house. I heard drug transactions and people fighting over drugs and alcohol all the time. I grew up watching and mimicking rap videos that glorify drug and alcohol use and abuse. Jerry Springer was a show that I watched often which was full of explicit content. I also watched any hood movie that came out (*Juice, Boyz in the Hood, Menace to Society, Belly, etc.*) These "programs" showed addiction on all levels, poverty up close and personal, and racism in our justice system. What I see right now is nothing like what I've seen as a child and young man. Financial education has changed my life in more ways than I can describe in this book.

My Unfair Advantage

My introduction to financial education came in the form of a book written by Robert Kiyosaki called *Unfair Advantage*. A friend that I met in prison had been released and sent it to me. From that day it changed my life. Learning the difference between assets and liabilities change my whole belief system. It didn't just change me financially, but personally as well. If you weren't an asset in my life, you were a liability that needed to be removed. I realized that only success could come into my life from this simple formula. Boy was I right! Immediately after I implemented this change in my life my financial circumstances changed and things began to fall in place. I acquired a barbershop and many rental properties that bring me positive cash flow and passive income.

I created another stream of income as a car salesman, which also produced positive cash flow through passive income.

Before I explain how this works, I need to educate you on some financial jargon. Jargon is best described as special words or expressions that are used by a profession or group and are difficult for others to understand.

Investing 101

Real Estate Investing is for Everyone

There are many ways to become prosperous from assets, so I don't want you to think that when I use examples that work for me that what I am suggesting is that these exact same things will work for you. That's not the case. Although, I stand firm on my opinion of the value and benefits of real estate investing. It is used by all the rich for tax purposes. So, no matter who you are or what path you choose, investing in real estate is something that I think everyone should learn the ins and outs of. If you're reading this book, I'm going to force-feed it to you, regardless. Starting now.

Cash Flow and Capital Gains

Cash flow is periodic amounts available to an equity investor after deducting all periodic cash payments from rental income. Let's break it down even further, for example: you rent out a house for $500 a month and your mortgage payment on that house is $400 a month. That means that the $100 profit is considered your positive cash flow.

Now that we have that down to a simpler form, let's focus on capital gains.

Capital gains are the profits on the sale of a capital asset (a property or investment) generally taxed at favorable rates. The deduction of capital losses against ordinary income is limited. Let's break this down, for example: if you buy a house for $50,000 and then turn around and sell that same house for $100,000 the profit of $50,000 is what you would call a capital gain.

Now let's explore the two major financial words cash flow versus capital gains. In real estate, these two words are like Democrats and Republicans. Generally, investors only invest in one or the other. For example, when you buy an apartment to use as a rental property you are doing this for an additional stream of monthly income. This is called investing for cash flow. There are many benefits that come along with investing for cash flow. We will cover those benefits in a few minutes, but right now I want to focus on the differences between cash flow and capital gains. Let's examine the current trend and try to figure out why so many people choose to invest for capital gains?

Capital gains investing is also known as flipping houses. I know most of you have seen the infomercials about how you can become a millionaire in real estate by buying for cheap and selling at a big profit. They also teach you about wholesaling which I will talk about in more detail later. Basically, wholesaling is like being a middleman. You find houses that are selling or in foreclosure for bargain prices and you find buyers that will pay market prices for these below market bargain houses and then you make a profit on the spread in between.

The Pros and Cons Between Cash Flow and Capital Gains

Each of these investing methods have benefits and risks, which is where the opposing views come from. I do not endorse one over the other or pretend to know what will work best for you. The world of finance can make it seem as if you must choose to pursue one or the other. This doesn't apply to me. All that I see and focus on are creating assets and shedding liabilities. I see profitability on both sides, I pay attention to what works just as much as I take heed to what does not. Allow me to explain:

Cash flow Pros

First Pro: Tax Breaks! This is what the wealthy use to become even more wealthy. The wise Robert Kiyosaki always says, "it is not about how much money you make it is all about how much money you keep." Taxes are the key to successfully investing in Real Estate. Many people think that Real Estate investing is all about renting out property or buying and selling property for a profit. Yes, those are major benefits, however taxes are a major loophole for the wealthy to keep the money that they earn through Real Estate investing. Cash flow is taxed as a form of income called passive income.

Types of Income

There are three types of income:

- Earned income
- Portfolio income
- Passive income

Earned income

Earned Income is money earned from a job as an employee. Earned income is taxed the most out of the three. The employee is taxed from their paycheck before he or she even sees it. Although President Trump lowered taxes, earned income is still taxed the most.

Portfolio income

Portfolio income is money from securities and other non-business investments like stocks and bonds. These produce dividends, interest, optional premiums and income from a royalty or annuity. Portfolio income has more tax benefits than earned income.

Passive Income

Passive Income is money acquired in any trade or business conducted for profit in which the taxpayer does not materially participate. Rental income dealing with real estate is passive income. Rental activities include long-term rental of apartments net leased property, office equipment and automobiles. In contrast, the rental of hotel rooms or transient apartments or short-term car rentals are not passive because of the extent of services provided.

Amortization

Second Pro: If you own a real estate property and you rent it out, you are an active participant in rental real estate and you are allowed to shelter up to $25,000 per year of losses against non-passive income. That's one tax break for cash flow but there are many more. You can also receive a tax break for something called amortization. Amortization is a gradual paying off a debt by periodic installments. You receive a tax deduction under generally accepted accounting principles (GAAP), the cost of an intangible asset is to be amortized (written off) usually over the life of the assets.

Depreciation

Third Pro: Depreciation is a reduction in the value of an asset with the passage of time, due to wear and tear. Let's pay close attention to this one because Uncle Sam is saying, even though your house may appreciate it will still receive a tax deduction for depreciation. You receive an annual tax deduction for the wear and tear and loss of utility of property. Tax Depreciation allows a tax deduction without a cash payment. Thus, providing an important benefit to real estate investors. The annual tax depreciation deduction allowed for improvements (land is not depreciable) is 3.64% for rental housing with a 27 1/2-year life; and 2.56% for commercial and industrial property with a 39-year life.

1031 Exchange

Fourth Pro: A tax break known as a 1031 exchange. This is not a tax deduction; this is a deferred tax method in which you pay the taxes at a later date. Section 1031 which is the section of the Internal Revenue Code (IRS) that deals with tax deferred exchanges of certain property defines general rules that you must follow. In a nutshell, this tax loophole allows you to sell property without paying capital gains sales tax if you reinvest those gains in more real estate of a like kind. You can do this until you die and the deferred tax will die with you. So whoever receives your real estate will not continue to carry that deferred tax, yet if you try to cash in on your house then you'll have to pay all the taxes that you didn't pay in all of the 1031 exchange's that you filed in the past. For example, if you do the 1031 exchange for an apartment building and your capital gains tax would've been $15,000, but now you have decided you want to sell your new property that you acquired through the 1031 exchange you just want your money so that you can retire and travel the world. This is when you must pay the previous tax of $15,000 from the tax that you avoided in the 1031 exchange plus the new capital gains tax in your present sale.

The government gives companies and investors these tax loopholes as an incentive for being a producer in our economy. By producer I am referring to fortune 500 companies who create jobs and real estate investors who create housing for the economy, they are producing. Most Americans will fall into the category of a consumer, a person who purchases good and services for personal use. Consumers bear the burden of tax because they are considered less valuable to the economy, consumers are considered liabilities. Producers get tax breaks as a reward for strengthening the economy. We are assets! This could be offensive to some who don't understand the gravity of our class system, however, this is the way of the world. So those are the four tax breaks (pros) in cash flow. Those are the pros. I know you're thinking that those are great, and you are right. There are a lot of benefits to investing in cash flow. There is one con though.

Cons of Cash Flow

Your profits will come slow. Steady, but slow. There are ways to speed things up, but we will get into that later.

Capital Gains Pros and Cons

Now that we have a good idea about cash flow, it's time for us to figure out the pros and cons in capital gains investing.

Capital Gains Pros

First Pro: Quick money! We all love money so that's why we get overly excited and motivated when we watch the infomercials promising to show us how to make a fortune by following their formula. It's very easy to flip your money and growing markets.

There are many formulas to get rich from investing in capital gains. A lot of people get rich from wholesaling.

Wholesaling

Wholesaling is a short-term business strategy that investors use to make big profits by finding homes that are about to go into foreclosure and matching them with a buyer. People can buy systems or research ways to find people who are about to lose their homes in the next 90 days. With this information they approach the owners with purchase agreements. They offer to help the owner avoid foreclosure by selling their home or buying their home for a profit. Let's say you got a loan for a home and the home cost $100,000. You've been paying on this home for 12 years and now you only owe $20,000 on the loan. You lost your job and now you were unable to pay on your loan. Your house is now about to be foreclosed on. You get a knock at your door one day and the person offers you $60,000 for your home. Pay attention here: remember you only owe $20,000. With $60,000, you will be able to pay off your home plus have an additional $40,000 for your pocket. At this time, it's a no-brainer for you because it's either go into foreclosure and have your credit all messed up or sell the house and walk away with a few dollars in your pocket. The man who knocked on your door that's the guy who's doing the wholesaling. He already has a buyer waiting to buy the house for $100,000. So, the wholesaler makes $40,000 on the deal.

Fix and Flip

Second Pro: Another way an investor can make money off capital gains is the flip and fix technique. This is where you buy distressed houses at below market value in areas where homes are selling at market value or above market value. This is where I shine! You can do this technique in many ways; however, my main objective right now is to explain the pros of capital gains. We will focus on techniques in later chapters. The profits in a fix and flip can be very prosperous.

Example: you can buy a distressed home for a purchase price of $20,000 in a neighborhood where houses are selling for $100,000 or better. You can take $10,000 for material and $10,000 for labor. That would be a total investment of $40,000. If you sell the house for $100,000 you now have a $60,000 profit.

So, you see how a person can make a lot of money from fix and flips. There are many ways to capitalize off capital gains so now that we have looked at the pros let's look at the cons.

Cons of Capital Gains

Taxes! Taxes are a major disadvantage for capital gains investing. This method of investing doesn't allow you to acquire and keep assets. Without assets you cannot protect yourself from inflation. You might have a lot of money, but with a dollar losing its purchasing power, your money and wealth can be stolen from you by the hidden tax called inflation. If you plan on leaving behind some assets for your children, then you will need to add a little cash flow to your portfolio. Investing for capital gains can also be a problem in a down economy. Just look at what happened in the 2007 recession. Investors were wiped out for investing in capital gains. When the recession hit, the real estate bubble burst and investors were stuck with homes that they couldn't sell. Its obvious capital gains can make you rich, just remember how important it is to protect yourself from these types of cons.

Good Debt Versus Bad Debt

These are the cousins of assets and liabilities. The proper use of good and bad debt is an imperative financial education tool that has been left out of our school system. These two forms of debt are what keep the poor and middle-class from becoming wealthy. First, what is good debt? Good debt would be debt that puts money into your pocket with pretty much the same definition as an asset. Although you use other people's money (OPM) to acquire assets.

Good Debt

There are many ways to use good debt to become wealthy. To be honest, good debt is the key ingredient to becoming wealthy. You will never meet a billionaire Who didn't use good debt to help them acquire their wealth. Learning to use debt to your advantage is financial education at its best. For example, good debt is getting a loan to purchase a rental property that will put you in debt but put cash flow into your pocket every month.

Here's an example:

You take out a $100,000 loan from the bank. You then purchase a four-unit apartment building at a 30-year mortgage. Your monthly mortgage is $500. You charge rent $500 per unit. That's $2000 in monthly passive income. Deduct the $500 for the monthly mortgage and you are now left with $1500 of positive cash flow.

You will have other expenses, but you get the gist of this example. This is good debt because the debt put $1500 in your pocket every month. Even though this sounds extremely simple, which it is, people are still afraid to do it because of their social programming. Their minds not being able to conceive that debt can be good. I know people with great credit scores and great yearly incomes who brag about them being able to go to the bank and get loans but won't. Why? Because they don't know the difference between good and bad debt. They know that if they can get a loan for $100,000, they will buy a new car, maybe a new boat or even a new house to live in. So right from the beginning the way that they think is liability based. This is not by accident. This was all part of the design. Our failed school system is why we don't have a clue on how to troubleshoot our own financial decisions. The elite made sure that the poor and the middle-class think through a liability thought process which leads us to what is called bad debt.

Bad Debt

This is what causes poverty, torn marriages and in extreme cases suicide. A lot of the time, credit cards are the number one cause for bad debt. People follow the old saying and "rob Peter to pay Paul". In simple terms, they use one credit card to pay off the other. Others even borrow against their own personal residences just to pay off the credit card debt and make their car payments. This takes them further and further in debt, because now they're home is at risk of foreclosure. This cycle continues until they file for bankruptcy. Then they start the process all over again in hopes of doing it right this time. Although deep down inside they know that they don't know how to be successful financially because they have never been taught money management or financial literacy.

Naturally they then begin to associate any debt to be bad debt altogether. They begin to avoid debt., Then their credit score rises, and their money begins to grow slowly. This is when most people become content living from check to check, saving for retirement in a 401(k). Once again this is how the Elite have planned to play this out, we get to have an illusion of security. You are living from check to check, having a liability state of mind, being in bad debt, and having an ancient educational system without financial education in the curriculum is all part of the plan. The elite want you to refinance your house to buy boats, cars, clothes, take trips, etc. This is all bad debt at its finest. We have even been tricked into thinking that houses and cars are assets by allowing us to believe these liabilities add to our net worth. The number one trick is making you think that your house is an asset. Remember the most important message in this book was the on the first page: Assets put money into your pocket! Yet your house takes money out of your pocket through property taxes, utilities and repairs, etc. This fact alone 100% makes your house a liability.

Equity

There is an exception to the rule: If you borrow against the equity (sometimes called real property value) in your house and use the capitol to build wealth. Then your house magically transitions from a liability to an asset through the proper use of good debt.

This leads us to our next two concepts:

Good expenses Versus Bad expenses: Speak the Language

Before I start on these two concepts, I want to explain to you why learning financial terms is so important. Every form of business has its own jargon. Remember from the earlier chapters, I explained that jargon is a word or phrase that is used for just that field. For example, in football they have a player who is called a quarterback. Unless you know football, you may not know what a quarterback is. Just like real estate... If I were to ask you what caveat emptor was, you would probably look at me confused thinking I was speaking another language. I'm not, it simply means, "let the buyer beware". The buyer must examine the goods or property and buy at his or her own risk. If you decided to buy a house and the contractor stated that it had *caveat emptor* and you read over it because you didn't understand and purchased the property anyway, this could end up being a disaster. Words are so important. It's like if you try to blindfold me and give me directions in Chinese to lead me through the hallway I would run into every wall in my path. If you speak English, which I understand, I will be a lot more successful navigating the halls. This goes for everything. I might be able to explain the basics of real estate speaking in layman's terms, but if I were to try to teach you advance strategies and techniques of real estate, it would be impossible unless you know real estate jargon. Let's look closely at these two words I mentioned earlier which are *good expenses versus bad expenses*.

Good Expenses Versus Bad Expenses

These items are also relatives of assets and liabilities. Although they are distant cousins, they still make it to the family reunion.

Good Expenses

First and foremost, good expenses are expenses that will protect your assets as well as protect your wealth in case of emergency. Such as life insurance, car insurance, house insurance, renter's insurance, car payments (not a Bentley or expensive car while you are on your grind), your home, utilities, healthy food, etc. I call these good liabilities because even though they take money out of your pocket they give back to your life in other ways. With insurance, it helps you stay wealthy if an emergency were to occur. It will allow you to hedge your money against future losses.

Hedging

Hedging is a strategy used to offset investment risk; to protect ourselves from losing or failing by counterbalancing action. For now, I'm going to continue to write out these definitions because I don't know how familiar you are with these terms. My goal is for you to know all these words. Together we are about to create a movement that will change our way of life for generations to come.

Ok! Back to business! I get excited and I tend to bounce around, so bear with me. Good expenses are supposed to be used as a hedge to protect your wealth. I know that this all seems like common sense and to be truthful it is. Yeah, it's something that we know subconsciously. We can feel when we are doing things right or wrong. However, the feeling most of the time comes after the fact. Just imagine, if you had been taught from elementary what and what not to do with your money just like they taught you your ABC's and that 2+2 = 4, it would be second nature for you to make sound financial decisions. You would know that a good expense would be paying a mortgage on a four-unit apartment that brings you monthly cash flow would not only be a good expense it would also be an asset as well. That is why they're all at the same family reunion. That is a very happy family. We must also look at the unhappy family members who has an immediate family full of bad expenses.

Bad Expenses

These are easy for me to name because I grew up around people who had bad expense spending as their way of life, including myself. We are a product of our environment, so I know this lifestyle all too well. The liability family with bad expenses are right there eating up all the food at the table but won't even pay their dues to attend the family reunion. Some examples of bad expenses are leasing a BMW with a high monthly car payment while still living in the projects on section 8; getting your nails done for $60 when throughout the month you barely have gas money to get to and from work. Bad expenses occur when you have 50 pairs of Jordan's, but your kids are on welfare unable to pay for their school lunch. I must admit, all of that was personal and these are things that I grew up around, I am sure some of you can relate. Bad expenses can also be expensive car notes, cable television with 500+ channels, eating McDonald's every day, expensive vacations, expensive jewelry, Rent-A-Center furniture, expensive mortgages that you can barely pay, payments on the latest cell phone when you already have last year's edition, buying new clothes when you still have tags on the ones in your closet, buying snacks at the store when you have a house full of food, etc. I could go on and on about bad expenses and I'm sure you can do that too although if you are like me, we have to stretch our thinking to come up with examples of good expenses. Not the rich, they have been trained from birth to recognize good expenses as well as good debt and assets. This is a cycle we need to begin to implement in our own household. Our children are the future so it's a must that we equip them with all the tools that they need to excel to their fullest potential. The only way for them to reach their potential is for us to reach ours first. We can no longer allow ourselves to live below our capacity because if you live below your capacity so will your children. Since our subject is financial education, we are going to take a trip back in time. We are going to look at the origin of money and help throughout history it has been controlled by the elite.

The Origin of Money

Agrarian age

This was a time when a person's tenure, their job, was farming in the fields. They used what is called a barter system.

Barter System

This is when you trade one good for another without the use of money. This can also be appropriate for services. For example, one cow might buy you 50 chickens. It would be an even trade if both sides felt it was an even exchange. The only problem was making the actual exchange. If I only had cows and I needed some chickens from you but you wanted deer meat, I would need to go to the man that has deer meat in hopes that he has a need for cows so that I could trade with him in order to trade with you. As you can see this was a hassle just to get the things you needed to live comfortably during those times.

Commodity Money

The people began to use other forms of valuables such as seashells, jams, stones, gold, silver, diamonds, etc. These are the first forms of currency, called commodity money. With this new form of currency, it became a lot easier to buy and sell goods.

Bronze age

Metals became the money eventually when men learned how to refine crude ores and craft them into tools or weapons. The metals themself became of value. This was the bronze age in which iron, copper, tin and bronze were traded between craftsman and merchants along the trade routes and add major seaports. This is how coins came into play. The only problem now was once a person began to collect a large amount of these coins and commodity money, they needed a place to store their money safely. This is where the origin of banks started. The goldsmiths back then who handled large amounts of precious metals and other commodities and their trades had already built vaults to protect their own inventory, so it was a no brainer for them to offer vault space to their customers for a fee. The goldsmith could be trusted to guard the coins because their coins and valuables were in the vault as well. When your coins were placed into the vault you would receive a written receipt which allowed you to withdraw at any time. At first you were only able to get the money from the vault, but after time, it became custom to issue not just one receipt for the entire deposit but a series of smaller receipts adding up to the same total. Each were printed across the top page of the bearer on demand slip. This was the first form of any modern-day checking account.

The Fractional Reserve System.

This was one of the biggest financial schemes ever created and it still exist today. Once the Goldsmith (the Banker) realized that most people who deposited the money in his fault never come to get their precious metals or commodities all they wanted was these pieces of paper (receipts) that the banks issued out, he figured since they keep their money in the vault that he would loan it out to other people with interest.

Interest

Interest is a payment in exchange for the use of money over a period of time. You can earn interest by lending your money to a bank. You pay interest when you borrow money from a bank. The rate of payment can either be a fixed amount or a variable amount throughout the lifetime of the loan or deposit.

For example: If you loan me 100 but when I pay you back you want 120 in return. That would be 20% interest. OK, well this is what he did with other people's money. (OPM)

Everything went fine at first until the banker (the Goldsmith) he gets greedy and loans out more than he has in his vault. Once this happens it's now called fractional reserve money. This trick still goes on today. Some banks have a fractional reserve of 1 to 40. Meaning that for every dollar you have in the bank they can loan out $40. Did you hear me? They take your one dollar and they make up $40 out of thin air and loan it to someone else. I know what you're thinking. We need to start our own bank! All right, back to the Goldsmith (the Banker) who loaned out more than he has in his vault. Everything runs smoothly until people make a run on the bank.

Run on the Bank

A run on the bank is when depositors want their precious metals and commodity out of the bank right now. Uh-oh, there is trouble now!! There isn't enough money to pay everyone their money back at once, so the bank then becomes *insolvent*.

Insolvent

Insolvent means unable to pay the debt. This is what happened in 2007 when the market crashed, and we went into a recession. We only felt a slight change because we have been living in a depression since birth. Now, we have discussed three forms of money: commodity, receipt, fractional and now last, but not least, *fiat money*.

Fiat Money

Fiat money is currency that is made legal tender by government law or regulation. In the United States, federal reserve notes are fiat money. The fiat money always has a legal value that exceeds its intrinsic value. Our dollar bill is fiat money. Was that definition of fiat money powerful or what? It states that we are forced to use this fiat money as legal tender. This means that you cannot deny this money for payment and it is against the law to do so!

Chinese Origins

China was first known to create fiat money in the 13th century.

This was recorded by Marco Polo during his travels to China...

"The Emperor's Mint then is in this same City of Cambaluc, and the way it is written is such that you might say he hath the Secret of Alchemy in perfection, and you would be right! For he makes his money after this fashion."

He makes them take of the bark of a certain tree, in fact of the Mulberry Tree, the leaves of which are the food of the silkworms, --these trees being so numerous that whole districts are full of them. What they take is a certain fine white bast or skin which lies between the wood of the tree and the thick outer bark, and this they make into something resembling sheets of paper, but black. When these sheets have been prepared, they are cut up into pieces of different sizes. The smallest of these sizes is worth a half tornesel; the next, a little larger, one tornesel; one, a little larger still, is worth half a silver groat of Venice; another a whole groat; others yet two groats, five groats, and ten groats. There is also a kind worth one Bezant of gold, and others of three Bezants, and so up to ten. All these pieces of paper are [issued with as much solemnity and authority as if they were of pure gold or silver; and on every piece a variety of officials, whose duty it is, have to write their names, and to put their seals. And when all is prepared duly, the chief officer deputed by the Kaan smears the Seal entrusted to him with vermilion, and impresses it on the paper, so that the form of the Seal remains printed upon it in red; the Money is then authentic. Anyone forging it would be punished with death.] And the Kaan causes every year to be made such a vast quantity of this money, which costs him nothing, that it must equal in amount all the treasure in the world.

With these pieces of paper, made as I have described, he causes all payments on his own account to be made; and he makes them to pass current universally over all his kingdoms and provinces and territories, and whithersoever his power and sovereignty extends. And nobody, however important he may think himself, dares to refuse them in fear of death. And indeed everybody takes them readily, for wheresoever a person may go throughout the Great Kaan's dominions he shall find these pieces of paper current, and shall be able to transact all sales and purchases of goods by means of them just as well as if they were coins of pure gold. And all the while they are so light that ten bezants' worth does not weigh one golden bezant.

{Ref: *The Travels of Marco Polo/Book 2/Chapter 24*}

I added this because it sounds ruthless and it is. Our fiat money system is almost parallel with that of China. In fact, after China, America was the next place in the world to adopt fiat money. So basically, the whole concept came from China.

Gold Standard

I'm about to fast forward in time a little since we are doing the history on money right now, I'm going to cap it off with the gold standard. There is a whole lot more history on the origins of money. I will have that book written for you soon as well.

In 1971, Richard Nixon took the dollar off the gold standard. But before we get into that let me first explain what the gold standard is. The *gold standard* is a monetary system under which units of currency are converted into fixed amounts of gold. Such a system is said to be anti-inflationary. The United States has been on the gold standard in the past. (In 1933 it was taken off but was also put right back on in the same year, 1933) in 1971 however, it was taken off once more. This is still the way as of present day. So, let's break this down. Back in the day when the gold standard was in place, for every dollar that was in your pocket it was backed by gold. That meant you could turn in your dollar and get gold in return. This made your dollar worth something. This also kept the government and the federal reserve from printing extra money. They were only allowed to print an equal amount of fiat money compared to the gold that they had at Fort Knox and the vaults. With this system in place, this kept the economy stable and it made the US dollar worth every penny. That is way back in the day when a nickel could buy you a whole loaf of bread. Try to follow me closely on this concept because this is extremely important. In 1971 when Nixon took the US dollar off the gold standard (remember Richard Nixon was impeached by the way) everything changed. The floodgates open wide! No longer were the federal reserve or the government required to live by the gold standard. They were free to print as much fiat money as they saw fit. This brings us back to the taxes and inflation (the hidden tax) and most of all ERISA.

ERISA

Employee retirement income security act (1974) also known as ERISA.

This act of 1974 was a law governing the operation of most private pension and benefit plans. The law eased pension eligibility rules, set up the pension benefit guarantee corporation and established guidelines for the management of pension funds.

OK, let's do our thing and break this all down. By now I want you to know when anyone gets to talking about rules and guidelines, they are setting things up in their own favor. In other words, they are stacking the deck so that all the good cards go to their hand and the losing cards come to us. With that said let's check this out. I must pause for a second because I need to bring you up to speed of what era we are in, The Industrial Era. (1865 - 1990)

Industrial Era

This is the era of factories. We were building cars, airplanes, railroads, oil companies, tobacco companies, etc. All these companies offer a retirement pension plans and other benefits. Well the ERISA act changed all of that. These industrial companies are no longer required to offer these retirement benefits. Then the domino effect began, and millions lost their retirement plans, causing many of them to have to go back to work. ERISA made the employee responsible for their own retirement plans. This makes ERISA the mother of the 401(k) plan, KEOG, and IRAs. Now all the money that you saved from your paycheck and invested into your 401(k) goes straight into Wall Street into the stock market. They give you the option to invest your hard-earned savings into high-risk investments or low risk investments. The high risk yields higher returns and low risk

46

yields lower returns. They want you to gamble with your money. Yet it's still someone else who's doing the gambling. It's the broker who is managing your money. He gets paid whether you lose or gain money. He picks the stock, bond or mutual fund, etc. that he wants. Basically, you are left with no control over your hard-earned retirement money. If he loses it all, what happens? Right. You are broke. He might or might not lose his job, but I bet you that he still has his money. All he needs is someone else to work for. Yet everything that you have worked for is gone and now you have to start over at 50 years old. This is why financial education is so important. Let's check out some more of these rules and guidelines. First, you were left with no choice but to send your hard-earned savings to the stock market. Second, this hard-earned money is taxed before you even see it on your check. So, this means you are investing money that is taxed already. Third, they will tax that same money again as earned income when it comes out during your retirement. This means that you will be getting taxed twice for the same money. WOW!! Fourth, yes there's more, if you need to use some of your own hard earned already taxed savings for something important, they are going to penalize you 10% of your money. Do you hear what I'm saying? They are going to take 10% of your already taxed money. This must stop! Wake up, this is extortion! This pains me deeply because I grew up around poverty all my life and I always wondered why no one could get ahead in life. I wondered why my family had to struggle just to pay the bills when they work their butts off to put food on the table. Then I would see the middle-class kids with newer cars, better clothes, etc.... But we all went to the same school, and they didn't live far away from the hood. Now as I look back, I realize that we were all in the same boat. You see, the wealthy are out of sight. They go to private schools or they are taught at home. Plus, their homes are somewhere hidden because I don't have a clue where they live.

Economics 101

Inflation Versus Deflation

Inflation is a rise in the prices of goods and services. Let's start with inflation since most of us have heard this word a lot but somehow it is so mysterious.

Inflation

All right let's get onto this inflation business. Let's see what all the fuss is about. Inflation happens when spending increases relative to the supply of the goods on the market. In other words, there's too much money chasing too few goods. That is a good definition although it leaves out that it's the greatest slight of hand trick that the rich have ever created next to the fractional reserve system. Now that was clever. If the fractional reserve system is king, and inflation is queen and taxes is the prince. Inflation is the silent killer because you can't see her coming. For example if you put $10,000 under your mattress right now and keep it there for 10 years that $10,000 would not be able to buy the same things it could buy today but just look at the price of milk not so long ago, milk cost anywhere between $1.80 to $2.25 a gallon. Now milk is anywhere from $3.25 to $4 a gallon. Look at cigarettes. They used to cost $2.50 now they are 6 to 7 dollars depending on what state you are in. In some states they are even more like New York where it can cost you up to $12 per pack of cigarettes. This is the hidden inflation tax at work. This is happening because the federal reserve, the government and the banks are printing money out of thin air. The more money they print the more inflation will rise. The trick is amazing because it appears as if everyone is getting richer with more money circulating in the economy. It's like playing Monopoly. The game runs smoothly with the bank and the amount of money that the bank hands out to all the players at the beginning of the game. Well, imagine if we opened another monopoly game and took the bank from that game and gave everyone double the money. What would happen? Would it change the game? And if so, how? Well, it would be the same old game except there would be more money and then the people would pay more for properties. It may appear that everyone has more money. Having more money does nothing but make the prices go up. Although in the real-world people work hard for this money and when prices rise because of inflation that doesn't mean that your paycheck goes up as well. If your paycheck stays the same and the price for everything rises, well that means life gets a lot harder. Because when this new money hits the economy is first used by the rich and by the time it gets to you, prices for goods have already risen. The rich benefit from the new money and you suffer when prices go up. When the money finally reaches you and things go back to normal, the people rejoice as if things have gotten better. That's inflation and its finest. Now it's time to look at her twin sister *deflation*.

Deflation

Deflation is the decline in the prices of goods and services. Deflation is the reverse of inflation. It should not be confused with inflation which is slowing down the rate of prices that are increasing. This right here is the definition of the economy in the hood. For example, to buy houses in the hood is easy because they are cheap. They're cheap because no one with money wants to live there or buy anything in that area. There's no money in the hood, so you won't see many stores, malls, plazas, etc. The only stores you might see our discount stores like Family Dollar, Dollar General and little corner stores. Now we all know that. If deflation were to go beyond the hood, what do you think would happen? If you said the people would panic, you would be

49

correct. That is not with the elite want. They would rather pump up the economy with Monopoly money than to let all of that happen. I'll tell you this though, we're going to change this cycle of deflation in the hood through acquiring financial education. I refuse to allow my people to remain in this state of being. Like I said before the only difference between the rich and the poor is what they know. This is why I am writing this book about financial education. I promise there will be many more to come. I will teach, study and learn financial education until my last breath. Our kids are the key to our future. If we can start teaching them early they will change the world. It starts with us first, so back to business, we have no time to waste. It's time for us to get to the meat of this book. We had to get the basics down first. I know that the history of money was something that most would think to be a little unnecessary. Yet it is my personal belief that in order to change or learn anything you must understand its origin. So, giving you a brief history of money was inevitable. It's now time for you to learn how to use these tools to your advantage! Don't worry I will walk you through every step.

My Journey into Acquiring Assets

Real Estate tax lien sale

This strategy of real estate is one of my favorites because you can purchase a house for as little as a few hundred dollars. This allows you to be able to invest in real estate when you don't have much savings in the bank. I never knew that deals like this existed in real estate until I met my mentor, Paul Andreozzi. I call him "Pops" even though he is white I still look at him like a father because our relationship grew to be that close. When I first met him, it was on bad terms. I had hired a few of his workers which were childhood friends of mine that I hadn't seen in 15 years. They borrowed his scaffold to fix the drywall in a duplex that I had purchased for 15,000 this was the first property that I had purchased upon my release from prison in 2015. I actually paid too much for this property. I purchased this property through a realtor and later purchased another house from him as well. The worker was doing a good job considering the type of work that I was getting done at the time. Just as the job was coming to a close I went to go let them in the next morning to finish the job and someone had kicked in the back door, stole the scaffold and cut all the copper electrical wires in the basement. I'm guessing they got scared of the electrical wires because the electric was live. I never found out who did this, but I think that it was an inside job. The workers immediately contacted Pops to let him know that his scaffolding was stolen. He arrived at the duplex in record speed. He was very angry and vowed to get to the bottom of it. I was even more angry because now I have to get the electricity rerun through the whole house plus I had to offer to pay for the missing scaffolding since it was in my house and we still needed one to finish the drywall job. Pops tried to refuse the offer but I didn't let him because I know that I was going to get to the bottom of this and get the old one back. The stolen scaffold (that I never got back) and the electric wires ended up being a blessing in disguise. Not only did I meet Pops, but I also met Uncle Ray. Ray Scalise, who I refer to as Uncle Ray, is the electrician who came to fix the electricity in the duplex. He did this with flying colors in one day for only $250. Me and Pops exchanged numbers, but we really didn't communicate other than updating each other about the progress on the stolen scaffolding. Then one day I saw him in an area that I just purchased another property for $7500 and I was so excited that I bragged to him about the deal and he chuckled and called me sweet. Not the good kind of sweet but the naïve kind. He told me I was paying too much money for the properties that I was buying. To me these were steals because the houses are stable and only needed cosmetic work. He said since you want to buy up everything, I got a house for you. This house was only two houses down from the one I just bought. Someone lived there so when he showed it to me, it had a tenant in it already. The house needed cosmetic work but it was livable he said give me $5000 and you can have it. My reply was I want it right now. He just laughed and said OK, But I'm taking you to the tax lien sale in a few months.

From that point forward we would talk to each other for hours at a time almost daily. He started teaching me everything that he knew about real estate. In the meantime, I had two properties and I was working on my third. I was working from 10 AM to 10 PM in my barbershop almost every day of the week. I nearly cleared $10,000 a month in the barbershop on most months and other days I would sell cars just to make extra money so that I could invest more money into real estate. Let's do the numbers on this real estate. The duplex I purchased cost me $15,000 and another $2000 to get both sides ready to be rented. I like to remodel kitchens and bathrooms of the properties that I purchased because normally that's what people look at when they are thinking about renting. The rest of the house is nothing but empty rooms. Paint and a little bit of drywall mixed with some new carpet or floating floors around the house and it looks brand new inside. Once it was completed I rented out both sides for $650 each. That brought me in cash flow of $1300 a month. In a matter of 13 months I had my money back. Let's do the math $1300 for 13 months is $18,200 deduct $600 for the property taxes I had to pay for that year and that gives me $17,600. From that day forward I have what is called an *infinite return*.

Infinite Return

An infinite return is where I get back every dime that I put into a property in addition to the money that it cost for me to purchase the property. After that every dollar that I collect is an infinite return. My goal was to purchase a property every month or every other month. I knew that if I acquired assets with all my extra money, I would build myself an empire in due time. Every dime that I made besides what I spend toward food and bills went towards acquiring assets.

My wife is amazing! Without her, I truly believe none of this would be possible, especially in the timeframe that we accomplished it in. She is my secret weapon and I'm like Superman with her by my side. The best way I can describe our connection and unfair advantage is that she allows me to be in two places at one time.

My First Real Estate Tax Lien Sale

This strategy of real estate is one that I suggest for anyone starting out because you can purchase a house for as little as a few hundred dollars. This allows you to be able to invest in real estate when you don't have much savings in the bank. I never knew that deals like these existed in real estate until I met Pops. By the time I got to the tax lien sale, I had a total of five properties: two duplexes and three single-family homes.

Doubt

Only the duplex and the single-family property that I bought from Pops was finished and rented out. The other three were being renovated. At this time, I was starting to have doubts, because although I was acquiring assets through real estate, I was always broke, and all my extra money went into my assets. Between cars, homes and materials, I just couldn't see a profit. Deep inside I knew that I was doing the right thing, but my pockets were singing a different tune. Despite what my pockets or anyone else thought, I knew that all I needed to do was push. I pushed, and it landed me in the Jefferson County Courthouse at my first Delinquent Tax Lien Sale.

Familiar Territory

Here I was ready to purchase some properties, the irony is that the sale was held in the exact same court room that I was criminally tried on several occasions and received sentences that totaled 16 years in prison. That room has been life-changing for me in both negative and positive ways. Before I entered the court room, I received a bidding number from a courthouse representative who I went to school with. We were both surprised to be seeing each other on these terms. I entered the court room with my briefcase, with my business attire on and ready for business. The first face I see is Pops. We quickly exchanged notes on what houses that we had our eyes on, we were given a list of all the addresses that were on the foreclosure list. In each case the owners had failed to pay their taxes. The last thing we wanted to do was to bid against each other. The time that you spend before these sales talking with other attendees, networking, could make all the difference in the world. Without that communication Pops and I could have spent our entire day waiting for a specific property to be call only to find out we were bidding against each other, in which case one of us would have backed off (probably me out of respect.)

Tax Lien Rules

Before the sale began they gave instructions on how the auction would be handled. On the list was the back taxes that were owed on the property which they identified with only the parcel number. The price owed was the starting price for the opening bid from that point on the bid could be raised by any amount until no other bids are made. Bidding wars are fun to watch it is like watching a ping pong match. Back and forth. Sometimes the real experienced bidders put on a show they will one dollar up the other bidder until your almost ready to fight, however it is just business. The last bid wins the property bid and from this point they will contact the original owner through mail or by phone number. The owner will be given 90 days to pay the past due taxes, after that the winner of the bid will be contacted. The winner of the bid will be given 30 days to pay and if he does not pay, he will not be allowed to participate in future tax lien sales. When you pay the amount of the bid the transferring of the deed process begins. After this process takes place which is usually is 12 weeks maximum. You are not allowed to enter the property at any time until the deed is transferred into your name, and if the house is occupied you'll have to be accompanied by the sheriff's department. The sheriff will escort the old owners or tenants out or you can come to some sort of rental agreement that either way you are in full control. This experience was life-changing for me. I won bids on three properties that day. Two single family homes and one duplex. I acquired two out of the three. I did not get one of the single-family homes because the owner paid his delinquent taxes within the allotted 90-day grace period. I paid $5000 for the duplex and 3000 for the single-family home. Both are in great shape. I was so happy after the tax lien sales that when me and Pops went to eat after I was bragging about the deals I got, and his reply was "I told you that you are sweet". I just started laughing. He was right. I had tons of book knowledge, but I was green when it came to experience. I was finally starting to get some skin in the game. It was as if all the pieces of the puzzle we're coming together thanks to Pops. That's why I called him Pops. He became a father figure in my life. The next lesson he had for me was the auditor sale.

Auditor Sale

This is pretty much the same as the tax lien sale. Whatever property houses or lots that are not sold will be up for sale at the auditor sale. The opening bids an auditor sale can start as low as a dollar. One common strategy is not to bid on the properties that you want at the tax lien sale unless someone else bids on it because of no one bids on it will automatically move onto the auditor sale where bids can start at a dollar. In my mind none of my readers can ever have an excuse for failure ever again. if you're reading this book you have no more excuses!

I just gave you a way to build wealth starting with a dollar!

Yes, you will need more than a dollar to get up and running, but it's a start and that's better than sitting around complaining about being dealt the wrong hand in life.

Accounting & Legal Matters 101

D.I.Y LLC Formation

Now that you have acquired your first property, the next thing on your list is to form an LLC to list on your deed. This can be done by accessing your states Secretary of State's webpage. For example, my state site was www.ohiosos.gov. Once on your site you will search for the Articles of Incorporation (Form 532A) my fee was $99 for filing. Now just like that in a matter of moments my LLC was formed. That was free game I just gave you, write this down or highlight it because I might have to charge for this later. All jokes aside, there are attorney's as well as wolves in sheep's clothing that will charge you anywhere from $100-$500 to form an LLC. It is as simple as checking your Facebook and searching for an old friend. I know most of you have done that once or twice. Ok, let's get back to it!

I am glad we took a moment to cover these steps, so you don't spend too much of your money before you start making it.

E.I.N Application

On that note: one last piece of advice. Once you have established your LLC, do not pass GO, instead go straight to the I.R.S website www.irs.gov and electronically file for your E.I.N number (this is a free service) By acquiring a business identification number you then have the ability to accept checks and money in the LLC name, which builds credit for your business name, you can open a bank account in the LLC name which allows you to keep your money separate for tax reporting purposes, and it also gives you an added layer of asset protection.

Protecting Yourself

In business you must be sure that you are protected from predators. When you begin to accumulate wealth there will be many people who want to steal what you have. They will come from all angles so you must in turn protect yourself from all angles. You'll need an attorney to help structure a cloud proof protection plan around yourself and all your assets. For example, although an attorney is not required to do this in real estate for each property that you acquire will need to structure an LLC (limited liability company) to convey the property and its name.

We spoke about LLC formation in the last section so be sure to follow those steps and save yourself some money.

Convey

Convey means to deed or transfer a title to another. To convey your property into an LLC protect you as well as your wealth.

Let me explain:

If you own a house in your name and god forbid something fatal happens in your property like someone dies because of a house fire due to faulty electric wires, your personal assets are protected from litigation.

A lot of the times when you have older homes, the electric might need to be replaced, but because it works just fine, you may think it's OK to keep it as it is. Then this happens. This scenario although extreme, would be an unfortunate event, but it could happen. Yes, your insurance will take care of a lot of the material things. However, if the house is in your name you can be sued for your personal items and unrelated assets as well. Such as your money, other investment properties, separate businesses, your personal accounts, your home, everything that has any value to put it short. Although if you have the structure of the home in an LLC, then they will only be able to sue the company and not you personally.

The Benefit of Multiple LLC's

It is important to have multiple LLCs, because the same thing could happen to all your investment properties. If you have all your properties structured under one LLC, you might not lose your personal property but all your investment property will be liable. However, if you structure an LLC for each individual property only that one LLC will be liable and your other LLC's will be safe. Asset protection is incredibly important when you are building your wealth. It's vital that you study financial education whenever you have free time. Financial education should have been taught to us as soon as we learned to count.

Making business money transactions are something that we all do every day. When we go to the store to buy gum we're making a money transaction. When we give someone a dollar or even lend it to them, we are making a transaction. We can go on and on about the different ways to lend, give, borrow, purchase, sale etc. with money. Money might not make the world go around but it is the fuel that makes it move. The million-dollar question goes back to the fundamentals: Why isn't Financial education a major part of our school curriculum?

By high school we should be financially literate. Our parents should already be living examples of financial education and should already be implementing a hands-on approach of our economic literacy skills so that by the time we finish high school, we are advanced. That way, if we do decide to become a teacher,

Dr., firemen, etc., we will know how to invest our money in ways that will build wealth and prosperity. The rich do not want this for the middle class and for the poor because it will close the gap of wealth giving them less control over the masses. It will even the playing field for our children and their children. Yet this is not the case and by the time that financial education is introduced to us it sounds like Chinese. When we first pick up a business plan or business law book or a finance book, it's like trying to learn a whole new language. But the rich kids are speaking the language fluently. They are ready for more advanced learning. What happens most of the time is that you revert to what you've been taught all your life. Just be a worker bee. Then you get those rich kids from school your money to invest while you take all the risk and they reap all the rewards. I know that I got off subject but it really is on point. I'm going to get back on track to asset protection. This just triggered how important this Education is for us. This goes right in line with our next subject because while you were in school you are not allowed to take test along with someone else. It's called cheating. And financial education however, working together as the number one rule to success and prosperity. And financial education you need teams, administration, as well as mastermind groups.

Your Asset Protection Team

First we need an attorney to help us with what the legal rules are in any faction of business that we may participate in. We will also need for our attorney to look over contracts as well as to form contracts to protect ourselves from predators who want what you have. I know that you want to believe that we live in an honest and truthful world, and we do for the most part. Although when money comes into the equation, most people change into someone that you don't know. If you don't believe me, try telling someone No when they ask to borrow money from you. They won't care why you can't lend the money and if that reason isn't good enough for them, they will crucify you right there on the spot. You are not allowed to do as you please with your wealth, you have to do what others want you to do with it. Yet they never ask themselves why they don't have the money that they feel like you have and why they are entitled to it too. Hiring an attorney will help you hide yourself from most of these types of people maybe not family and friends, but most predators will be kept at bay. Now as far as family it will be our job to teach them financial education and money will never be a problem.

The Tax Attorney/CPA (Certified Public Accountant)

Your CPA is vital to your growth financially. He will also help you structure the right entity to put your company under.

Entity

Entity is the legal form under which property is owned. The benefits and risks of owning a business or property may vary depending upon the entity that is formed.

The Different Types of Entities

- Corporation
- S-Corporation
- Sole Proprietorship
- Joint venture
- Limited Partnership
- Partnership
- Tenancy in Common
- Joint Tenancy
- Limited Liability Corporation
- Limited Liability Partnership
- Real Estate Investment Trust (REIT)

Your CPA will help you choose which one of these is best for you as far as your taxes are concerned. Your attorney will also help you pick and entity for legal asset protection. So together with those two you will pick an entity for whatever it is that you are doing. If you have a business, depending on the size and employees you might want to form a C- Corporation or if you're self-employed you might choose an S corporation. Although LLCs are the most common because of its asset protection firewalls. Others can be useful as well. I am no expert, so we will have to hire the experts to do this. This is why we need an asset protection team. They will help us get all the right answers. Our next team member will be for real estate. This is our realtor.

The Realtor

A realtor is a professional in real estate who subscribes to a strict code of ethics as a member of the local and state board and of The National Association of Realtors. This member of the team will help us find homes within our budget. He will sit down with you and figure out what your budget is and what type of real estate you are looking to purchase. There are two types of property: commercial property and residential property.

Commercial Property

These types of properties are designed for the use of retail, wholesale, office, hotel or service uses. This type of property is usually for business. They even have a division in the bank for commercial property lending. Apartments with more than four units are considered commercial property as well.

Residential Property

Residential property in real estate brokerage terminology, this means owner – occupied housing. In income taxation terminology, rental units are used for dwelling purpose, not of a transient (hotel or motel) nature. To qualify as residential, at least 80% of the building's income should be derived from dwelling units. We are more than familiar with this kind of property since we most likely live in this type of residential property. Single-family homes are usually three bedrooms or better, two-bedroom homes are for smaller families and one-bedroom homes or apartments are usually for couples or someone who lives alone. Each of these dwellings have different advantages and disadvantages. There are also apartments, duplexes, triplexes and quads. These all have advantages and disadvantages as well so when you sit down with a realtor you will go through all these types of investments to see what is best for you.

Once you determine your budget and category that you're going to invest in, he or she should set your phone up to receive notifications so that you are alerted every time a commercial or residential property is listed on the *M.L.S.*

M.L.S (Multiple Listing Service)

This is an association of real estate brokers that agrees to share listings with one another. The listing broker and the selling broker share the commission. The M.L.S usually furnishes its members with a book of all the listings that they published online updating the book or online data frequently. Perspective buyers benefit from the ability to select from many homes and any member broker. There will be photos for you to look at for almost every section of the property. It will also give you the purchase price, age of the property, capitalization rate, comparable properties, etc. We will go over all of this and upcoming chapters. All this information is vital and important when shopping for an investment property. A realtor will also help you get funding to purchase these homes as well. The good thing about this team member is that he is free. He earns money from commissions. That means he only gets paid when the house or property is sold. Next on our asset protection team is the property management team.

Property Management

The operation of property as a business including rental, rent collection, maintenance, etc. are included in property management.

The following tasks are often required in the ownership of property. Property management tasks include:

- Accounting and Reporting
- Leasing
- Maintenance and Repair
- Paying Taxes, Utilities and Insurance
- Remodeling
- Rent Rate and Collection
- Acquisition and Disposition
- Development and Rehabilitation Feasibility
- Financing
- Income Tax Accounting.

There are some people who don't want to deal with all these tasks, so they will hire a property management company to do all of this. As other businesses grow to a bigger portfolio, they will hand over their responsibilities to a property management company.

Portfolio

This term describes a combined holding of more than one stock, bond, commodity, real estate investment, cash equivalent or other assets by an individual or an institutional lender. The purpose of a portfolio is to reduce risk by diversification. A bigger portfolio will require a close watch because it will become easier for big and small tasks to slip through the cracks. You can't afford for things like this to happen because they will begin to hurt your cash flow in a major way. With this in mind, hiring a property management company at 10% is a great option. This is especially true if you own property that is in another state or a great distance from where you live. Your next team member is your banker.

The Banker

In most cases you will have multiple bankers. This is because you will want to use other people's money as much as possible. Banker's will help us fund our portfolio, but in most cases, we will have to meet the requirements of the bank. For example, if you wanted to purchase a duplex for an investment property, you would first have to fill out a loan application with a loan officer. Their job is to get all your financial information as well as the information on the duplex that you are trying to purchase. They will want full disclosure of your financial records for at least two years and your tax returns, also your *debt to income ratio.*

Debt to Income Ratio

This is how much you make each month minus your monthly expenses. For example, if you make $10,000 each month and your bills plus all your other expenses add up to $3500, then your debt to income ratio is 35% banks usually require less than 36% so you are good. You will also be required to have at least a 720-credit score. The duplex may also be required to have a *loan to value* of 90 to 95%.

Loan to Value (LTV)

LTV is the amount that you were going to borrow compared to the value of the property. For example, if you're going to purchase a duplex for $100,000 and you are asking for a loan for $80,000 then your LTV would be 80%. It also looks great if the duplex is worth more than the purchase price. That makes the LTV in your favor even more. After you fill out the loan application, the loan officer will send your application to the *underwriter*.

The Underwriter

The underwriter is the person who ensures another or takes certain risks. In mortgage lending, this is the person or company who approves or denies a loan based on the property and the applicant.

In securities, it's the broker that sells the issue and, unless sold on a "best effort's" basis, agrees to purchase the shares not bought by the public.

Ultimately, they are basically the ones who approve or deny your loan based on what the bank has as requirements.

These are some of the insurance requirements that we've already covered:

- Debt to Income Ratio
- Credit Score
- LTV
- Two years proof of income from your W-2's.

The next team is the heart and pulse of our real estate business which is the master builders of construction.

Construction 101

Master Builders of Construction

This team is the pride and joy of our business. For more reasons than one, not only does it make the family rich, construction business also provides jobs for so many men and women. With this team, we will change the structure of low-income housing across the nation. We will rebuild our community one house at a time with top quality workers who have been building since they were in the playpen. We will hire all first-tier workers who have skills in roofing, framing, drywall, painting, electrical, HVAC, etc. We will even hire unskilled laborers who can help with cleanup demolition and other things. We will be able to train them in a skill. Our master builder army will build houses from the ground up. We will also specialize in Rent Ready projects.

Rent Ready Work

Rent Ready's are properties that other owners rent out to tenants who need repairs after a tenant has moved out. We will have a master builder construction team that focuses on remodeling homes in low income housing using the WAHM (Webb Affordable Housing Model) strategy that was designed and mastered by who I refer to as the teacher, James Webb. He is the founder of the master builder construction. His techniques of being able to take tier workers off the streets and supply them with work to help them support their family plus rebuild the community that they grew up in. That's a sure way to success in all aspects so let's examine this WAHM strategy a little further.

WAHM (Webb Affordable Housing Model)

As I mentioned earlier, the strategy was formed by a great man, James Webb, who I had the honor to work with while serving in Butner Federal Medical Center located in Butner, North Carolina. He was falsely imprisoned for trying to uplift black communities. He made the mistake of not protecting himself against the big predators who are the same predators responsible for the lack of financial education in our school system. I met Mr. Webb at a real estate class he taught in the educational department at Butner. At this point in my life, I thought I had a pretty good idea of what real estate was all about, boy was I wrong. I knew the basics that was it. I knew about cash flow and capital gains, and I knew a little bit of asset protection, but that was it.

What I did not know was the language. I couldn't speak it fluently although I could understand it clearly. The first time I went to the teachers' Master Builders Class he talked about construction which was like a foreign language for me. I knew a little because I had to do all types of repairs on my properties and it took thousands in losses before I learned through trial and error how to spot a good worker and how to tell if a worker was just milking the clock. Although I did have workers that could get the job done. Sometimes I found myself having to go back over the same job because of poor quality work. At that time, I didn't realize how little I knew about construction and how the business side of things worked. One thing I learned about myself is that I hate to be clueless about something that I should know about. Yet when it comes to construction, I was clueless to even know that this was something that I needed to know. When I went to the teacher's class I rejected it as not even relative to real estate but he had a projector in his class where he had pictures in a book that he had written with him standing in front of a mansion, a Bentley and an LF 150 with blueprints in his hands he also claimed he had made millions in real estate. So even though I had no interest in what he was talking about (construction) I couldn't get those pictures out of my mind. I wanted to know how this was possible in construction.

The next day I decided that I would talk to him one on one to get a better feel on this dude. Before I even said a word, my mind was made up that he was going to feed me the same old prison talk as I'm all too used to hearing. As he began to talk, he went right into the WAHM strategy. He was speaking the financial language that I love so fluently that it knocked all my walls down. As a matter of fact, he was so well versed, that I had to give him my full attention just so that I could comprehend what he was saying. As I listened, I realize that I was being introduced to a whole new strategy of real estate. What caught my attention was the uplifting of the poor communities. From that point forward I knew that I had to turn into the student if I was to learn everything the teacher had to offer me.

Here is a letter from the teacher about our time together:

I heard that there was a brother who had arrived at FMC Butner who was very brilliant and who had a nice real estate portfolio of around 20 rental homes and who had good knowledge in real estate and business. Having taught many classes in Real Estate and Construction along with other courses, some of my former students mentioned to me that I needed to meet Brandon. I invited him to sit in one of my classes and from that day forward we both became iron sharpening iron in our friendship. While I had met and taught some pretty sharp brothers B was much different. I soon realized why. While construction was new to his volumes of knowledge, it did not take long for him to start to master principles of construction too. A teacher himself, B had a drive and thirst for knowledge unlike I had seen from other students. Literally hours upon hours, many times 9 hours straight, except for quick food and other small breaks B was studying.

His thirst for knowledge was not just for his own benefit, but it was as if he was daily planning and visualizing an empire he was soon to build with his wonderful wife and children, all engaged. B taught everything he learned in construction to his wife who shook the nation of wives and other prison family members who on Wednesday nights taught each other principles of construction on phone conference calls based on the same weekly curriculum that the men were learning in my classes. Tonica, his wife was just like B, who was all about action and making things happen. B was proud of his mentorship as the pictures came back in and not only did the family's construction business grow but no local construction manager was needed as all of B's master builder friends were inspired to actually see Tonica on top of the house roof giving directions to the workers. The Crawford Family has grown and is growing up the most brilliant and beautiful young women and kingly men who will change the world. While they say I have inspired them, both Brandon and Tonica have truly inspired me and I am sure as all of our irons continue to sharpen each other's irons the world will welcome our leadership, as we all bring about positive changes to the lives of many.

James T. Webb
The Original Master Builder

WAHM Meaning

The teacher explained what WAHM means, it is the Webb Affordable Housing Model. The program outlines a method of buying homes in low income areas with comps, which is short for comparable or comparable sales properties that are like the ones being sold or appraise. Comps that range from $50-$75,000. These are the areas that we are targeting. We want to find distressed homes in these areas that we can purchase at $10,000 or less, then put 10,000 into the home for repairs and materials and another $10,000 for labor costs. That is a $30,000 investment. Then you turn around and sell the home for $65,000 to first-time homebuyers through FHA loans (FHA 203B, farmers loans, VA loans). You end up making a $35,000 profit with this system and everyone is happy.

Renters in Low Income Housing

This will allow people with lower credit scores of 680 and below and a high debt to income ratios as well as people who are currently working for housing rather than using the last two years of W-2's. This gives low income people more flexibility. If they can purchase a home for $65,000, this will not only help people build their credit, it will also help them begin to build assets and wealth. It will also however, help with their monthly finances. Whereas if they were merely renting, they may have a rent payment of $700 per month. Now their monthly mortgage is $460 per month. This is a win for the low-income community altogether. They receive a fully renovated home with new roofing, electrical, plumbing and HVAC they will take care of these homes because they are the owner. The neighborhood will rise in value because all the homes have been renovated and updated. The homes are also for owner occupied purposes now as well. The city will be free of eyesores, so everyone is happy.

CRA Credits

The bank is happy because now everyone has assets on their book and they also get CRA credits. *CRA credits* are community reinvestment act credits. This is a federal law that requires federal regulators of lending institutions to encourage lending within local area of the institution. This applies particularly to low- and moderate-income residents and those residing in inner-city neighborhoods. As of right now there is also a new tax rule that is meant to help distressed areas.

Opportunity Zones

These areas are called *opportunity zones* and considered domestic tax havens that were created under the Republican Tax Bill the president signed into law. Through this rule an investor who rose capital gains into an opportunity fund can avoid up to 50% of their taxes otherwise owned on those investment gains. The investor never pays taxes on any of the gains the fund accrues on its investments in the opportunity zones. This is provided that the investment is held longer than 10 years.

Draft Regulations

The *Draft Regulation* reassures investors will still qualify for long-term tax benefits even if they invest in an area that loses its opportunity zone status in future years. It gives an investor 30 months to begin improving any property they buy within an opportunity zone. The Draft Regulations, which will be subject to 60 days of public comment would allow individuals, corporations and any other types of business to invest in new opportunity funds. The funds could only be seeded by capital gains such as the proceeds from selling a home or a share of the stock at a profit. 90% of the fund's investments must be in qualified opportunity zones the business counts as being an opportunity zone if 70% of its tangible property is there. In some cases that can lead to a fund holding only 63% of its assets inside an opportunity zone.

The workers are also very happy because they are loaded with work and this makes the community happy. The community now takes great pride in the areas that they live in. This also makes the cities happy because first they were able to collect their payments for property taxes a lot more easily which also allows them to collect their allotted *millage rate*.

Millage Rate

This is another tax rate applied to property. Each mill represents one dollar of tax assessment per $1000 of assessed property value. For example, if the millage rate for property taxes in Steubenville school district is 20 mills, a home assesses with the value of $100,000 pays $2000 a year in property taxes to the district. The city is also happy because when homeowners are owner occupied, the people are more prone to stay for the long-haul. This strategy will do more than just uplift you and your wealth; it will build up everything around you as well.

I know that anything takes practice, practice and more practice. I'm challenging you to study financial education daily. First, you need to buy your Barron's dictionaries. (This covers real estate terms, business and economics, finance and investment terms or anything else you're trying to learn.) Learning the complex language of real estate and business finance is essential to being successful in these fields. As your vocabulary grows so will your comprehension. This will allow you to become more advanced and intern make you a whole lot richer. You will get richer and richer simply by becoming smarter and as you become smarter you will work less as well.

Be Inspired

I hope this book helps you see how important financial education is for all of us. Especially now in the information age. With technology, the world is right there in the palm of your hand... Literally. Your smart phone! It gives you access to unlimited information and data. We will see billionaires spring up from all over the world, and they will come from all walks of life. With the Internet, you can market and sell things all over the world, whereas before you needed major capital to market and sell your product anywhere.

Limitless Thoughts

Success is In Your Mind

It all starts with how you think. Your thoughts are more powerful than you can ever imagine. Have you ever thought about somebody you haven't seen or heard from in a while and all the sudden you bump into the same person somewhere or you get a call from this person?

This has probably happened to everyone more than a few times throughout our lives. Well that isn't a coincidence. Our thoughts travel and they put circumstances and or situations into motion causing your thoughts to manifest in the flesh. This may sound weird, but our thoughts were working the same way as radio waves or the same way that your cell phone allows you to talk to someone on the other side of the planet. Your thoughts travel through the air just like radio waves, soundwaves etc. all these things move in vibrations on different wavelengths, but we aren't about to get into all that right now.

My point is that our thoughts create everything that you see with your eyes. Stop and think about this for a moment and look around you. Your clothes, watch, house, car, the cement you walk on, the chair that you are sitting on or whatever you're sitting on, etc. These are all first created in someone's mind. So with all of this said, I want you to take a clear look at the way that you think and know that everything you see in front of you and where you are in life, it's just a sum total of your thoughts. This is a universal law just like if you put your hand in fire you will get burned. If you stay underwater for too long you will drown.

The Secret

If you think negative thoughts, you'll attract negative things into your life. Although, the opposite is also true, if you think positive thoughts you will attract positive things into your life. This is what we called the law of attraction. I know you might be thinking what does this have to do with financial education. It has everything to do with financial education because for you to become rich and the physical, you must first create those riches in your mind. Even if it's by accident, like hitting the lottery. It is those numbers that you picked that won the lottery! Even if you see those numbers on a cereal box, you gave those numbers life through your thoughts and then you commanded these very numbers to bring you wealth. That's how powerful your thoughts are! The highest level of financial education goes beyond physical wealth. True wealth will be gained in a perfect balance of wealth, mind, body, soul (both mentally & physically) and spirit. Every one of these attributes are wealth manifested through you in the physical. With this wealth we will take back what is rightfully ours... Wealth and privilege on all levels!

The way that we think is the only thing that separates us from the rich and gives the elite and unfair advantage over the poor and middle-class. The way that we think is a product of our education. We are then further programmed to think certain ways through subliminal messages like TV, commercials, ads, billboards, radio stations, etc. Everywhere we look we are being influenced on what to eat, think, wear and do. We are constantly being monitored on how we think by the things we purchase, our reactions to changes in prices, how we use information that is given to us. It's so bad now that our phones can predict where we live by the number of hours it sits in one place and where we are headed by the routes we take while we are traveling.

The Mental War

The newest technology is incorporated with the education that the rich kids are learning. This allows them to keep the unfair advantage they possess over our children. We are fighting a mental war that most people don't even know exists. Financial education will not only make you wealthy, it will level the battlefield between the minds of the rich poor and middle-class.

Three Principles of Personal Finance

I hear people say that everyone can't be rich, but to that, I say, why not? They assume in order for there to be a winner there must be a loser, after all someone has to be the worker bee and that is a great point, however just because you are a worker bee doesn't mean you have to be poor. Just because you have a job doesn't mean you can't build wealth. It's not the way that you acquire money that makes you rich anyway, it's what you do with the money once you have it that makes you rich. This can either be the secret to wealth or the recipe for remaining poor.

Know the difference between these game changing principles:

- Assets versus Liabilities
- Good Debt versus Bad Debt
- Good Expenses versus Bad Expenses

These fundamental principles are the foundation of our secret education. Let's use the extremely progressive country of Dubai and their whole economy. Most of their population both the rich and their worker bees live luxurious lifestyles. The poor seem to be nonexistent in their country. The ideology that the United States or any other country must exploit the worker bees to have a balanced economy is simply not true. Everyone can live in wealth. It's just that the rich don't only want the wealth, it's the power that comes with the wealth that they don't want to share. They know that if everyone becomes wealthy they will lose their power to exploit your need for survival. They will lose their power to divide and conquer. This means they will no longer be able to cause wars due to lack of food and shelter. They will no longer be able to adjust the crime rate to how they see fit.

As financial education is taught and understood life as we know it will begin to change all across-the-board. Let's reflect. Ask yourself these questions:

- Do you see why the elite have left financial education out of the school curriculum?
- Do you see why financial education is so vital to our success?

Fear the Duct Tape

We must change the way that we think and the only way for us to do that is to challenge ourselves to think outside the box as

Shari Jo Watkins says:

"Fear the duct tape, never get inside the box. Once you get in the box someone can duct tape it shut, and you will never get out of the box. Think before the box!"

We need to fight for our freedom of thought, literally. Until we do this we will never be free to live the way that we want to. If we are not free mentally then our physical lives and mindset will remain limited as well. The saddest part is that most people don't even know that they are being programmed to think a certain way. That means they don't even know that they are in bondage mentally. Most people will think that something is wrong but just don't know what. As a result of this thinking, our people feel trapped so physically they remain trapped in the hamster wheel headed nowhere fast. This stops now!!! We will awaken through this knowledge so that we can enlighten ourselves first then our children. With this completely understood, over stood, it's time for us to get back to business. Next, we are going to find out how to read the market of real estate and business, the two go hand and hand. You cannot have experience in one and not the other and still expect to be successful.

Housing Markets 101

How Do You Spot Emerging Markets?

There are the four phases of a market cycle:

- Buyers' Market Phase 1
- Buyers' Market Phase 2
- Sellers' Market Phase 1
- Sellers' Market Phase 2

It's important to understand that the average time for a market to complete a full cycle will vary from 10 to 25 years.

Buyers' market phase 1

You'll have to be careful in this phase, because it's easy to find markets with an overabundance of properties. There might be too many properties being built. The amount of properties is at the top of the list of reasons a market will move from a boom to bust. How do you know if the market has too many properties being built? Well, we can determine this with precision. All we need to do is go down to the permit office and see how many permits are being requested. It usually takes a few years to plan, get permits and build a property. When real estate is booming, builders and speculators (Spec-speculative- Houses built without a buyer/user) take out a huge number of building permits. By tracking these permits you can watch out for markets that are at a greater risk of over building.

Jobs in the Market

Jobs can affect different market phases of real estate. In a buyers' market there are not many jobs. This causes people to leave the area. When this happens property value starts to decrease, the houses become cheap to buy and decrease in value. Property will continue to get cheaper and cheaper if the job market continues to shrink. This will not always be the case, but it might be like this for a decade or more.

Tax Abatements

This is usually when strong leadership will begin to come in and start offering incentives like tax abatements (abatement is it reduction in amount or intensity. This usually applies to decreases in taxes or rent) to businesses and corporations to encourage them to bring growth to the area by building factories, or headquarters like Amazon is doing now. What Amazon is looking for now is a location for their second headquarters. Large cities make great attempts to attract these large corporations because of the inevitable contribution to the city's economic growth. They plan to bring 20,000 jobs ranging from $50,000-$100,000 or better, so a city will offer low interest or no interest loans to companies. They may even offer free land.

Check in with the city leaders to see what they are doing to grow the city. If they are not doing or talking about doing anything to help jumpstart the local economic growth, then don't invest there. There are always plenty of markets to choose from. You just have to do your homework. This is called doing your due diligence.

Investing in a Buyers' Market Phase 1

In this phase you are basically investing in for cash flow. This will allow you to make a profit until the market changes. You must know how to do this correctly if you are not from the area and don't know how things work.

Economic Base

You must study the market to find out with the economic base is. An economic base is an industry within a geographical area that provides employment opportunities that are essential to support the community.

For example:

Steel production is the economic base for Pittsburgh, Pa. For each steel worker added to the economic base, there is another job added in a service employment. This could be a position as a Lawyer, Switchboard Operator, Barber, etc. Each new job is projected to bring two people to the community, this could include the spouse, children, non-working parents, etc. Once this occurs the total population will increase by four for each new job in the basic industry.

By knowing what the economic base is you will be able to predict what the future holds for this area.

Buyers' Market Phase 2

This is when businesses and corporations start to take the city up on offers and now jobs are in abundance. People begin moving to an area on a constant basis. To the point where the apartments and housing becomes full. Now property is starting to appreciate (increase in value). Even the most distressed properties in any given neighborhood are being bought up and rehabbed to get back in on this boom.

Investing in a Buyers' Market Phase 2

This is where you can make huge profits. This is also where you must keep a close eye out for any bargain available. Ask yourself, do you want to buy and hold until the market is right? If you sell too fast you could miss out on huge profits. One huge indication of positive change is when you begin to see new construction. This is when you know for a fact that the city expects an economic change. Think about it no government would invest millions into construction of new roads and highways if they did not forecast an economic surge in growth. You don't want to continue to buy when you see new construction because you will have already missed your opportunity in phase 2 of the buyers' market and now, we are entering the Sellers' Market Phase 1.

Sellers' Market Phase 1

This is the point where it's time to start unloading all the property that you've been acquiring for the past few years. Outside investors are coming in to buy as new construction is beginning to pop up everywhere. Now less and less properties are becoming available to be put on the market because as soon as it hits the market they are sold within a day.

Investing in a Sellers' Market 1

Soon as this happens the buyer's become desperate and start to engage in a bidding war. Everything in the market starts to rise and rent amounts start to climb, there's new construction on raw land, employment, and wages included. Everything is so high that even in the hood (urban areas) properties are selling for a nice profit. Prices are so crazy that speculators begin to appraise houses for more than they are worth. This is the time when we pull back from buying anything. Some may still choose to invest but we have made our money, and it's time for us to find a new phase.

Sellers' Market Phase 2

This phase represents extremely high-risk investing. Business and job growth have slowed so properties are not selling like they were. Everything has slowed down so much that properties may sit on the market for years at a time.

Investing in a Sellers' Market Phase 2

Now there are too many properties to choose from, when before you were lucky to find a house on the market. Sellers are becoming so desperate that they are dropping prices in order to get a sale. This is not a market that you would like to be in. Both job and population growth has slowed. To be direct, once all of this occurs it's time to move on. Now comes the fun part. Together I will walk you through a complete rehab of a property from the bottom to the top.

Property Rehabs

The property rehab is something that should be mastered. We discussed this concept earlier in the book, now it's time to get down to the details. We reviewed and discussed how we could purchase property from a tax lien sale for a few hundred dollars. Remember when I told you about buying property for as low as one dollar from an auditor sale. The one thing that can get costly when purchasing property this way is the repairs that may be needed to get these properties rented or sold. You gamble when you acquire these sorts of properties because you are not allowed to enter or inspect prior to buying. The one thing that you can be certain of is that no matter what issues the house has once rehabbed it will produce cash flow.

The Crawford Method

Initial Inspection

First, when we walk into these properties, we will have to secure them. That means we're going to have to buy new locks to make sure that it is safe and to make sure that all the windows are secure. The basement will be the deciding factor for me because if the basement is solid then we can fix everything else with no problem. We can fix the basement too, it's just a lot less of a hassle if we don't have to. If the basement is leaking, then we may have to put in a French drain, or we may have to restructure the foundation either way we will get it fixed for a bargain price. Our master builders can fix any problem. The basement will be a great indicator to a lot of repairs needed throughout the house. From the basement we will be able to identify any issues with plumbing. We will be able to see what condition the distribution board, more commonly referred to as the electrical box or electrical panel, is in and if the wires still run throughout the house. We will also be able to see what shape the furnace is in. The takeaway here is that on initial visit to a potential investment property your first thought should be let's go to the basement.

Utilities

Our second step after evaluating the basement is to see if we can turn the utilities on. We will most likely replace electrical wiring and piping throughout the house, unless it has already been updated, it's important to look at the areas of the house that affect the utilities. Nine out of ten times we will need new plumbing, new HVAC, new electrical, new kitchens and bathrooms, don't be afraid... We can get all this done piece by piece and we will get it done by a master builder and fund our ventures with the profits from our master builder construction company. We will get into this in more detail as well, but for now we're going to focus on the details of renovating our new rehab house that we have just acquired.

Plumbing

Plumbing Is the next thing we look at. While we were in the basement we noticed that some of the community crackheads stole all the copper pipe out of our house. Now we know that we're going to have to replace the plumbing throughout the whole house. Not a problem, we will replace the copper pipes with new PVC or PEX water lines. PVC is plastic and they are cheap and of no value to the crackheads so they won't bother these pipes in the future. PVC is so cheap the for the materials you will only need $150-$250 max to plumb the whole house. The downside of using PVC over the more expensive PEX alternative is that PVC does not expand so if your property is vacant or poorly insulated your pipes may freeze. When water lines freeze, they must have room to expand because once the frozen line thaws the pipe will burst. Pex line is a little more expensive and requires an $80 tool for installation, but it is easy to install and can with stand freezing cold temperatures without cracking or bursting your pipes. Keep track, this is your money after all, now you have about $250 invested in materials.

Plumbing Labor Costs

Labor for the plumbing is the next thing to consider. We will need to call one of our many plumbers and get an estimate for the jobs ourselves just like we do for customers in our construction company. Their rate of pay will be about $20 per hour and it will only take him one day to run water lines throughout the whole house. Yes, one day with a helper at about $10 an hour. This will equal out to about $240 for the total labor. This means that now the whole house has all new plumbing for a total of $490. Now that we have water we will work on the electricity.

Electricity

Once we realize that electrical wiring is old and outdated, usually knob-and -tube wiring, also known as K&T, we can assume this is a fire waiting to happen. A huge drawback to K&T wiring is that most insurance companies may deny coverage because of the perception of increased risk. Other companies will not even rewrite homeowner's insurance policies if K&T is discovered in the home unless K&T is completely replaced, or a licensed electrician certifies that the wiring is in good condition. Keep this in mind when purchasing older homes. Remain calm when you go through your house and you see the electric panel is so old that it looks like Thomas Edison installed it himself, you can handle this. Now it becomes a must to replace all the electrical wiring in the house including all the outlets. Material costs range from about $500-$650 depending on where we get our materials. We can safely estimate $650 for the materials.

Electrical Labor Costs

Next, we need to call one of our many electricians and again we are going to estimate the job ourselves the same way that we estimate for our construction company. Our electricians' rate of pay will be $25 an hour and it will only take him a day and a half max with a helper at $10 an hour. So that's a total of $420 for labor. Now we will have all new electricity throughout the house for $1070 including materials and labor. Once we have electricity after the plumbing, we can really get to work.

HVAC

Typically, the furnaces we see are so rusty that if you touch them, they may crumble and turn into dust. No problem! We're going to install a new one along with an AC Unit anyway. This will be our most expensive fix because a new furnace will cost around $500-$650. The AC unit will cost an additional $650. So together with the furnace and AC materials you've invested $1300 in material with a little extra that may go toward plenum's and transition pieces but that is a conversation for our HVAC Magician, Tyrone Davis.

HVAC Labor

For the HVAC labor we're going to give him a flat fee of $1000. HVAC guys bring skills to the table that will not take them a long time but require precision and care, so he will earn every dollar that he is paid.

I hope you are still keeping track, with materials and labor combined we will have a total of $2300 invested and we can rest assured our house will be cool in the summer and warm in the winter.

Gas Service

Now that we have heat, AC, electric and plumbing, we can check to see if the gas works. If not the gas company will handle this. All we need is a line to run for the furnace and the hot water tank. After all this is in place, we have all the utilities up and running and now it's time to start to do the cosmetic work. We're going to start with the bathroom. This is where the real fun begins!

Bathroom: One and Done

At this point in the renovation we have all our plumbing done and our demolition workers have already gutted the kitchen and bathrooms. By gutted I mean they cleared out the bathroom cabinets, vanity, old toilet, or shower or tub, stripped up the flooring, etc., it's now just a shell. Be sure to plan for power access if this is a new build and bathroom facilities because you will not have access to a toilet for a while.

A quick snapshot would look like this:

...we would run all necessary plumbing and wiring for bathroom fixtures; frame the area for the tub and or shower wall; Prep the walls for moisture resistant drywall (green board, which is actually purple) and or tile depending on the design; Paint and caulk where needed; install lighting; install flooring (tile, vinyl, laminate); install fixtures (tub, toilet, vanity); then Voila!

We will have replaced the whole bathroom. Toilet $50, vanity with mirrors $120, shower and tub $400, new floor $150, Materials will add up to be approximately $720.

Bathroom Labor

Labor for the bathroom is a three-day job and this will only cost us about $600. We will pay a flat fee to get this done. This is what we will always do. Although we estimate our pay on the workers expected rate of pay that we establish and document during the screening process. In this case for three day's work we would pay someone $20 an hour for 24 work hours to finish the whole bathroom. The cost of our completely brand-new bathroom would be approximately $720(materials) plus $480 (labor) we can estimate $1200. This is a great price because the value of your house will increase by thousands of dollars. Next, we are going to fix all the walls in the house.

Drywall

Beautifully finished drywall will change the entire look of the house. We're going to fix any holes that are in the walls or any wall that is uneven. Our goal is for the walls to be flat and smooth throughout the house. That means this price may vary depending on how many places we need to hang and finish drywall.

For example:
Let's just say that we need 20 boards of drywall hung and finished. Drywall, sometimes referred to as sheet rock, will cost about eight dollars a board (4 x 12) materials will cost about a total of $160. We will have a total of about $180 in materials because we will need to buy a bucket of mud as well.

Drywall Labor Costs

Once again, we will call in our master builders and hire our tier one drywaller and a helper and pay them $15 a board to hang and finish the drywall. This will cost a total of $300 for labor. This will also be done in a day or so for a total of about $460 and your house will look brand new aside from the floors which we hold off on deliberately because we wouldn't want our floors ruined during this process. Flooring is what we will focus on after we paint the house.

Paint

This will be easy since we don't have anything in the house. We tape all around the windowsills and cover the floor with canvas' or drop cloths. Then the painters will transform this house into a thing of beauty.

Kitchen

Like the bathroom, the kitchen is a focal point of the house. When the kitchen and bathroom are done to perfection, the house becomes an easy sell or a desirable rental. New cabinets, flooring, a backsplash, an island, and beautiful faucets make or break a kitchen. To renovate the kitchen can be expensive if you get creative and choose to go with high end fixtures. Yet following "The Crawford Method" we can renovate the whole kitchen for next to nothing and still make it look like a $20,000 kitchen.

Kitchen Labor

Our master builders yearn to show their skills in the kitchen and bathrooms because this is where most of their work shines and it is the easiest to do. We will pay them based upon their expected rate of pay and this job shouldn't take more than three days max when two contractors are working at $15 an hour for three days. That cost is about $360 plus the cost of materials you choose to buy to make the kitchen appear lavish. I estimate a total of $3000 maximum.

Don't Quit Before You Get Started

As you can see getting a house up and ready doesn't take as much money as the fixer upper show on HGTV makes it seem. Yes, there can be more things than what I covered that are needed to complete a house, but this covers the basics. Everything depends on what the house needs, every house is unique and different just like us. Yet with some tender love and care matched with creative thinking; you can turn a mediocre kitchen into one that is fit for the royal family.

Do or Die

I know that I've been making statements of how easy this stuff can be and I still stand behind that. Know that it takes a lot of diligence and hunger for knowledge to make all of this truly easy. You must apply this knowledge you are learning. You must believe in yourself, trust your hustle and grind like your life depends upon it.

Think about this:

What if the doctor told you that you only had one year to live unless you made $1 million with no criminal activity?

What would you do then?

I know what I would do: I would study, listen, watch, learn… and then execute! Flat out! I would be so focused that I would probably have multi millions when that year was up.

I know one thing I wouldn't do is go back to school. I would seek out knowledge from millionaires, seminars, personal resources, etc. I would be seeking financial education, not the traditional useless education that I learned in school. If I relied on that education to get to a million, I would be dead at the end of that year.

Be Unstoppable

Yes, that example is a bit over the top, I merely wanted you to see the type of focus that I'm referring to. If you truly want something and you focus all your being on achieving it nothing will stop you!

For Example:

Just think back to the time when your back was against the wall and you had to use every one of your brain cells so that you could make things work out in your favor.

How did it turn out for you? (Really take a moment to reflect on this because making these changes for you will require some self-accountability and that starts with changing your mindset)

Yeah, that's the grind I'm talking about. Studying real estate, business and accounting all fall under financial education.

Creating Generational Wealth

Be the Plug: Nepotism

Congratulations, since you have made it this far in the book, you are officially knee deep into the financial education that it takes to change your entire life! This is going to be hard at first, however as you learn the language and formulas in each field it will begin to become fun. I promise! Who doesn't love making money? Following "The Crawford Method" of investing you will begin to make money in your sleep, literally. The real estate and business world will start to look different to you. You will begin to see opportunities everywhere and in every interaction.

The most beautiful part is that you will begin to teach your loved ones and the people around you through your personal example. The way you talk, see and think will change. They will see it and want a piece of what you have. Now because the game was given freely to you pass it along to them and refer them to this book so they can have access to the same knowledge that you have and begin to break those generational curses in your extended family as well.

Look at you! Despite all odds! The one they may have given up on, being the change that you wanted to see in the world! This is a proud moment; you are seeking a secret education that has been carefully hidden from you your entire life!

Strength in Numbers

For me to say all of this is easy sounds good and it is true. Logically like we all know the plant must grow roots in the dirt before it can bear fruit for to us eat and feed others. That's why I call this process "Getting it out of the mud".

Do you know what happens when plants grow next to one another?

The plant's roots become interlocked. This makes the soil rich and fertile promoting growth.

I say this to you as a reminder, we need each other to grow stronger! Yes, you can grow on your own, you are doing this right now as you read this book, but you will never reach your highest potential without the support of others.

Elite Forces: He Who Has the Gold Makes the Rules

The rich know this concept and that is why the Rothschilds, Rockefellers, Morgan's etc. linked up together as a unit to form institutions like the Federal Reserve (FED), G.E.B board, the I.M.F and the World Bank. They knew that by themselves they could become wealthy but together they could control all the money in the world. Remember, "he who has the gold makes the rules." These wealthy families are the ones who have created the matrix we live in today.

The Invisible Influence

The elite have tracked the masses to the point that they deliberately market influences that without interception force us to believe that we smoke cigarettes because we are stressed or that we drink alcohol to calm our nerves. We have been programmed to smoke and drink alcohol. We are even programmed to eat certain foods, like the southern comfort food or soul food. Which by the way is the unhealthiest diet of all? We believe that diabetes, cancer and heart diseases are hereditary and in some cases they may be. However, in most cases these unhealthy eating habits have been passed down from generation to generation. Who is going to sit here and lie about loving Grandma's sweet potato pie or Auntie's famous mac & cheese?

The elite have people working in think tanks every day for their entire lives figuring out algorithms and patterns to use to trick us into following the trails of our predecessor's and maintaining a sheep mentality. The smartest psychologists on the earth come up with strategies to control the masses by using technology to make us believe they are protecting us and saving us but from who... Ourselves?

Un-natural Resources

It's crazy because the elite take and claim rights to the earth's resources like water, oil, electricity, gas, etc. Then they turn around and sell it to us. They don't purify the water themselves they don't frack the oil out of the ground, they don't build dams or erect electrical plants. The people do all of this. Why are we paying for it? This is a perfect example of how they have tricked us to believe in the illusion of power and tiny piece of paper, the almighty dollar!

Delusional Dollar

We believe that money makes the world go around. What if every dollar on the face of this earth vanished? What would happen? Would the world stop spinning? No, it wouldn't. Sure, there would be panic because of our belief in the almighty dollar is so deeply rooted. The masses would be lost at first, but then we would adapt. We would still know how to build homes, grow food, make clothing, manufacture cars, purify water, frack, create electricity, etc. This is a question for you to ask yourself: What point am I truly trying to make?

Your Mind is the Master

The point that I am making is that we are the money! We created money to serve us not for us to serve it! Do you have to be the master of money for it to serve you? No! Just like you must be in control and the master of your own life or you will be a slave to your circumstances and the will of others. I know that I'm getting deep and philosophical on you, however it's a must that we wake up and get out of this matrix. We must unlock our capabilities and return to our roots together and rise to our fullest potential so our children can grow even bigger and stronger from the first fruit that we bare. The work starts now!

The Recipe

There will be changes, and they need to start with us. *The Secret Education of the Rich* doesn't just refer to financial education. It starts with the morals, values and principles that are taught from birth. We need to be walking examples in the communities that we live in. The rich know that the soil (environment) that they raise their seeds (children) in will have a tremendous effect on the type of fruit (wealth) that they bear. These are key factors to the secrets of the rich.

The rich know that for their children to have an unfair advantage over the rest they must create an alternate destructive environment for the other children. First, they must infect the minds of the parents through the grandparents and great grandparents etc. Once we get all the way down to the newborn child the toxic environments are already created. This is the type of soil that I grew up in and it is not rich with nutrients it is instead poisoned with toxic waste. As a result, the seeds struggle to grow to their fullest potential. This in turn causes the seeds to grow and bear unhealthy fruit. This is what is going on all around us and as you read this it's happening to your children. It doesn't matter your color or race in most instances, although of course there are exceptions to the rule.

Let me explain:

The rich want to stay in power and retain control of the masses in the world. They want to do this by any means, this world is already divided into different races colors and creeds, although the elite of the rich are usually a predominately solid race. Throughout history the elite have been various races (Egyptian, Roman, etc.) at different points in time and the control tactics have been similar or the same.

Genetic Inequality

The Caucasian or white race represent the elite of today. I'm not picking on the white race, because all races have had their share of destruction, greed and active roles in poisoning the minds of the masses. Through the advancements of technology and the fear of extinction of the white race in the form of interracial reproduction countermeasures have been taken by encouraging the racial separation that has occurred over the past few years. The recessive gene in the Caucasian race mutates when mated with another race almost always darkening the skin color. Now no matter the shade, any sign of melanin in a person in our society qualifies this person as a member of the African American race. Remember the previous section from this chapter: *Strength in Numbers*, if the minorities become the majority tables will turn. The elite have become ruthless with their power and control tactics to prevent this change in dynamics. I'm not speaking racism because I truly believe we are all one race, the human race!

Although, I am speaking reality, and African Americans have been treated the worst of all groups during the period of time that the Caucasian race reigned as the elite power, it started from slavery and still exist today through racism and police brutality. The black community's soil is barren. It barely has any soil at all. The place I call home has soil that is rocky and dry, and it's generally referred to as the concrete jungle.

The Forbidden Fruit

It is impossible for seeds to grow properly without the right soil. If you can follow my comparison, you will realize my point that children need a conducive environment to have a chance at becoming successful in life. Some of the seeds fall through the cracks and reach fertile soil, through intervention of friends, family, church members, or mentors of any kind, but usually once the influences become stronger their roots are smothered and have a hard time growing surrounded by concrete. Through all odds it is a miracle that a lucky few still grow and bear fruit. I represent this exception to the rule!

One thing that our parents did right was bust up the concrete enough, for more of us to fall into those cracks. As our parents suffered the consequences of their actions through poor health, in old age, death and most commonly incarceration, we got to see firsthand what was at the end of the road we were traveling. The most fortunate of us through mere circumstances had angels intervene in our lives as guardians, mentors or coaches, etc. The wisest of us children, trusted our instincts and fought the influence and fell through the cracks and defying the odds. My two sons are great examples of this. They would prefer to play video games over hanging outside with friends in the dangerous projects they were raised in. They were sheltered from the influences and held accountable throughout their young lives even in my absence. They too will follow my footsteps and represent the exception to this rule because the outside living environment they were raised in produces killers and gang members. Guess what happens when the numbers of us ones who became productive increase? We become stronger!

For Example:

A Redwood tree can grow from a seed no bigger than a tomato seed to a tree that is as tall as a 35-story building. If a tiny seed can manifest itself into a grand structure because of good soil imagine what you can do!

When plants and trees grow in forests, they interlock their roots making powerful connections between one another and an environment rich in nutrients. This causes their seeds to grow stronger and healthier.

Look closely at what I am saying because this doesn't just apply to the black race, this is for humanity as a whole. When we interlock our roots together, we become stronger and richer which is why I chose this plant analogy, our children can grow stronger and should have the same opportunities regardless of race. We have all been so brainwashed, me included, that we separate one another by color when we are ultimately one race. Our different colors have no meaning they were decided by the environment that our ancestors migrated to in ancient times. We are all from one origin and epitomize God in the flesh.

It Starts at Home

Divided We Stand, United They Fall

Now you see how the elite knows this and use these concepts to exploit us, they use our colors to divide us, even after they divide us into races, colors and creeds, they divide us even further into social classes. The poor, the middle-class and the rich. A change has begun because there was a time in recent history when minorities were non-existent in any class, we were just slaves.

The elite made a terrible mistake. Their greed caused them to unite the masses in a common struggle of survival. The middle class is shrinking causing more people of all races to enter the class of the poor. When people become hungry, they will no longer see a color barrier all they will care about is food, clothing and shelter. In this state of mind people will begin to push for a change. A great example of this was the election of the first black president Barack Obama.

Massive Success

The elites only hope now is that we don't discover the importance of financial education. Well, guess what? It's over for that! I will shine the light on the importance of Financial Education until I am dead and in the grave. *The Secret Education of the Rich* has now been exposed. We will build universities with Financial Education as the core curriculum. We will teach each other how to leave generational wealth to our children. We will build universities that will teach hands-on ways to generate positive cash flow.

Access to The Secret Education of the Rich will be a momentum shift toward true equality. When you level the playing field in education, everyone gets a fair chance to spread their wings. This is what we're going to do before we end the book. I know that I've covered a lot and crammed in a lot of information in this one book.

Please understand that it's impossible for me to give you everything that you need to be fully educated regarding *The Secret Education of the Rich.*

Stay Tuned

You know what that means right? You guessed it, there are more books to come. As I learn, I will continue to teach and write out those teachings for you and future generations. It's amazing to me how much of our history is revealed through the history of money. If you study the history of money closely, you will see that the progression of all history is recorded in the transition of every form of currency. It doesn't matter what country you go to, follow the money and it will reveal everything you wish to know about that country 's history.

Talk the Talk

Learning the language of accounting is extremely important as I have mentioned all throughout this book. If we teach our children, the language of accounting from an early age they will be able to forecast any business with just a glance at its financial statements. They will be able to effortlessly pinpoint the exact location where a company is lacking. Our children who are brought up learning this financial education will be capable of running a Fortune 500 company straight out of high school.
I can hear you some of the naysayers now:

B, why don't you start a school now and implement this so-called financial education to enlighten our children?

I know for a fact that this would help tremendously! The answer to that question would be: Stay tuned! Our economy will flourish with this influx of intellectual and financially educated entrepreneurs. Our country would have the ability to reinvent itself as an "Economic Superpower of the World".

Beware

Although these positive changes would happen without a question. The elite would still reign supreme. You may be wondering:

How would they still reign supreme if we implement these teachings of financial education in the school system?

Isn't this the unfair advantage they have over us in the first place?

I'll explain, yes this is the main thing the elite have over us however this is not the only advantage they have.

Do you see now why The Secret Education of the Rich is not taught in schools?

Do you see why our children learn from a teacher who only makes $30-$60,000 a year instead of the money makers of the world who could be considered masters in the subject?

Sadly, it is safe to assume your child's teacher doesn't have a clue of how to apply financial education effectively into their own lives, let alone teaching these fundamentals to a class full of children.

Homeschooling

I have started to homeschool my children, specifically to reverse the mental limitations this ancient classroom style teaching has placed on my children by attempting to categorize them by grades and academic abilities. Realistically, some of the most influential people in the world were mediocre or poor performing students. By teaching all kids in the same way you are dooming the ones that have a different learning style. They typically never catch up and spend their lives exhibiting destructive behaviors to fill that void that was created when society showed them through their grading system that they were not good enough.

When we teach and monitor our own children, we ensure that no child is left behind. The elite teach their children financial education themselves by using real life examples through their own existing businesses. Their parents are the best teachers on earth. Generally, these teachings have been engrained into the minds of the elite families for generations. This education cannot be found in traditional school textbooks. This is your textbook! Our education is taught through application.

Muscle Memory

I know this might sound unfamiliar to some, but the actions of our parents are what molds and shapes our lives. If you really look back throughout your life, you will see that you are a 75% replica of your parents' image if not more. This can be reflected in your speech, if you are like me you randomly catch yourself using some of the same words your parents used. The things that used to irritate them when you were growing up now irritate you. The similarities are endless. Think of how you clean your house, fold your clothes, the spices you use to cook your food and especially how you raise your kids. This directly resembles how your family or whoever raised you did things. I know that there are exceptions to this, yet for most people this rings true in their lives as well as the lives of everyone they know.

Even though our social programming would have us reject this kind of comparison. I can hear it now, "I'm nothing like my parents," Yeah, you're wrong! On the flip side, the elite embrace this reality and intentionally walk in the same steps as their forefathers.

Do as I Do

You may have heard your parents say, "Do as I say, not as I do!" This is mental abuse! How are we expected to emulate something that we do not see at home? Even the things we despise about our parents are programmed in our minds as knee jerk reactions or unconscious coping mechanisms. Have you ever done something and immediately regretted it, thinking why did I do that? This is a prime example of unconscious learned behaviors from our parents or the people who had the greatest influence on our lives. The rich are fully aware that their children are watching their every move, so they use this as their greatest teaching tool.

For example:

Why do you think people like Nikes?

Do you think it's because that Nike swish is the greatest design ever drawn?
No. It's because we see everybody else wearing them. From a child we see the best athlete's and our favorite celebrities wearing Nikes, our parents, friends, etc. We immediately attach

self-worth to outwardly things. If you don't agree with this, take a trip to Goodwill, or GW Fashions as my wife's late grandmother would say, and pick out the most run down shoes you can find and wear them to the 4th of July family cookout and watch your entire family forget that they know you. They might begin to question your mental health they are certainly going to question your pockets, by that I am referring to how much or how little money you have. This explains the phenomenon of the two-hour waiting game that happens outside of footlocker every other month when the new Jordan's drop even though the identical shoes were already released 10-15 years ago. If you are part of the small population of the world who can care less about Nike, like my son Braijon, who only buys Jordan 1's in every color then I would bet my last dollar you are buying another brand that you've seen others wear.

Subliminal Warfare

The elite players of the world know all of this.

Who do you think controls the images we see on television, billboards, iPhones, etc.?

Not only do they use this form of teaching with their children, they use it on us as well. It's time to wake up, we are being played and controlled by people that you may never see before. Education is the equalizer. Education will level the playing field. We must continue to join at the roots and ensure that our seeds are planted in fertile ground.

I have compounded a lot of information and knowledge into this book, and I still have only scratched the surface on each topic. It's up to you to study each topic thoroughly on your own. First, you must learn the language. Then, digest the content so that you can use what you've learned to help you grow rich in every facet of life. Before I close, I want to leave you with one last challenge.

Win/Win Situations

Everyone prospers when we create win/win situations. This universal law applies to everything in our lives. If you create a situation where everyone involved wins and walks away happy this is a win/win situation. This pertains to business and personal life. In business, this is the way to structure a perfect business deal every time. Nine times out of ten, this sort of dealing will lead to long-lasting business relationships. Even in cases when you are prone to think I will take this one on the chin and get ahead next time. Avoid that urge and challenge it right away because it will be the beginning of the end for what could have been a great match. The win-win situation applies to everything. In marriage if one person always wins in every situation, how long do you think that marriage will last? If you want to grow in all aspects of your life, including family, marriage, friendships and business, I recommend that you take this universal law seriously. By creating a situation where only one side wins you give the competition a way to come in and you risk losing a potentially great client or opportunity.

This formula creates success in life. If you have a business and you create environments where you constantly generate win-win situations for both you and your employees, how do you think they will perform for your business? Excellent, everyone loves winning. When they're winning, they won't be late getting to work because they won't want to miss a chance at winning again. Who doesn't want to be on the winning team? If you can create win/win situations repeatedly in your business your company will thrive.

You will make this a way of life. Now when you go home and create the same win-win situation in your household paired with financial education and pure love, your home will begin to breed royalty and blessings straight from God! Your love and understanding will be centered and based on the teachings of God! Ultimately you will craft your lifestyle to one where you symbolize God in the flesh!

Challenges

Thinking with a win/win mindset is difficult for most because it's natural to think what's in it for me?

Our culture teaches us:

- *If you want something we have to go out and take it*
- *To look out for #1*
- *This is a dog-eat-dog world*
- *It's the game called life... win by any means*
- *It's a race to the top*
- *Friends, peers, strangers and family are all competition.*
- *The more they win the less there will be for you.*

Of course, we try to make it look good by cheering them on to be successful, although on the inside and behind closed doors a lot of us tend to be jealous when others are achieving things that we would like to achieve. Yes, great things have been accomplished from a determined soul! However, the greatest of accomplishments come from the one who mastered the "Art of We".

Communication Through Conversation

We as humans yearn to be understood by others. To have a voice that is heard, respected and valued. Most of the time we listen to respond rather than to understand. Conversations occur on a two-way street be sure to follow the road signs and communicate effectively. Move others by getting your point across clearly. Do not allow your message to get lost in the delivery. The best way to influence others is by affording them the opportunity to influence you. Most don't care how much you know until they know how much you care. Be vulnerable and express your true intentions and you will never have regrets. By refusing to practice these suggestions toward efficient communication, you are being what my sis, Tierra House, would refer to as a Volunteer not a victim. You can no longer claim to be a victim of circumstances when you are voluntarily ignoring the wisdom sat out for you. Share this book and this knowledge with everyone you know. I learn best through teaching so if you have gotten something of value in this book that can inspire change in your life, move forward and on your journey consider dropping a few lines in a book to encourage me as well as future generations to come.

Conclusion

I'm saying all of this to say this... The key to our growth and internal everlasting wealth is through one another. If we seek to understand one another, we will find riches of unimaginable quantities, right there in the hearts of others. Remember that money is just a piece of paper. It's our belief in that paper that makes it valuable. The real money lies within the people and that is the basis of The Secret Education of the Rich.

"The illiterate of the 21st Century will not be those who cannot read or write, but those who cannot unlearn the many lies they've been taught to believe."

~Alvin Toffler, American Writer, Futurist & Businessman